COUNTRY MUSIC'S GREATEST LINES

LYRICS, STORIES & SKETCHES FROM AMERICAN CLASSICS

BOBBY BRADDOCK

ILLUSTRATIONS BY CARMEN BEECHER

THE
History
PRESS

Published by The History Press
Charleston, SC
www.historypress.com

All illustrations for this book are by Carmen Beecher, including the one of legendary songwriter Harlan Howard on the cover.

All songs with lyrics featured in this book are published by Sony ATV Music Publishing. "Till I'm Too Old to Die Young" is co-published by Jumping Cholla Music, and "Southern Voice" is co-published by Round Hill Works.

First published 2020

Manufactured in the United States

ISBN 9781467146487

Library of Congress Control Number: 2020930494

For my Nashville family: Lauren, Jim and Dock.

—BOBBY BRADDOCK

For my daughter, Suzanne Gibbs, a true country music lover
who enthusiastically encouraged me in bringing the songs to life.

—CARMEN BEECHER

CONTENTS

WORDS

I have fond memories of long-ago lunches around Nashville's Music Row with small groups of songwriters. Inevitably, someone would make a decent new pun or say something profoundly original. If the legendary Curly Putman was present, he would snap to attention and cock his head to the side with a gleam in his eye and a hint of a smile on his face as he pointed his finger at the one who had uttered the clever words. Many times I saw Curly react that way when a potential song idea surfaced in conversation. It was his way of saying, "That sounds like it could be a song," and it often resulted in a co-writing appointment.

There are some very pretty melodies in country songs, but country music is best known for its lyrics. So while some country songwriters are tunesmiths, more country songwriters are wordsmiths—and quite a few of us are both. As a decades-long inhabitant of Music Row, I know a lot of the stories behind the songs and have had the privilege and honor of stumbling into more than a few songwriting sessions where music history was being made. I often thought that those attention-getting lines that are an important part of country hits would be an interesting topic for a book, and eventually I decided to try to make it happen.

I envisioned opening that book and seeing a story behind the song on the left page, accompanied by a related picture on the right page. The book's pictures would be lifelike drawings. I knew just who to approach: an old friend, world-class illustrator Carmen Beecher. I invited her to collaborate with me on this project, and it is my good fortune to have her on board to help bring these stories to life with pictures of the songs' characters or writers or singers.

Because so many country songs have crossed over into other fields of music and become important parts of our culture, I think there are few people who are total strangers to the truly American art form of country music. By featuring songs and song lyrics that span the early days of country radio to present-day downloading and live-streaming on the Internet, hopefully there's a little something here for everyone—an illustrated brief history of the words of country music and the songwriters who created those words and made them sing.

AUTHOR'S NOTES

I have previously written about my life in the music business. This book is about other songwriters, their great songs and some of my favorite lines from those songs. Although I often put myself into these stories as an eyewitness to music history, the focus here is on their works and not mine.

I want to thank the following first readers, listed alphabetically: Martin Bandier, Malcolm Gladwell, Chapin Hartford (my proofreader), Lauren Braddock Havey (my daughter), Tammy Jacobs, Michael Kosser, Kathy Locke, Suzanne MacKillop, Sharla McIver, Jay Orr, Don Schlitz, Carolyn Snider and Troy Tomlinson.

Because of copyright issues too complicated and boring to go into here— and also as a matter of convenience—for the most part, I'm featuring songs from the catalog of my music publisher, Sony/ATV (which in 1989 bought the catalog of my original song publisher, Tree International). There are so many great songs and song lyrics from other publishing companies ("Long Black Veil," "Good Old Boys Like Me," "Girl Crush"—I could go on and on and on), but I thought the vast Sony repertoire would be sufficient because it includes the works of some of the best songwriters and most famous artists/ writers of the past seventy-five years. The senior coordinator at the Sony music library in Nashville, Michael Worthley-Seldon, was an immense help in gathering information.

I mentioned my friend, superstar author/journalist/podcaster Malcolm Gladwell, as a first reader, and I owe him a further debt of gratitude for bringing *Country Music's Greatest Lines* to the attention of David Steinberger at Arcadia Publishing, who in turn brought it to the attention of its imprint company, The History Press. And I am very grateful for the help of acquisitions editor Artie Crisp and the History Press team in helping make this a book to be proud of.

Last but not least—actually most of all—I want to thank my friend Carmen Beecher, who surely didn't know what she was signing on to when I asked her to be the illustrator of this book. I wanted someone to bring my picture ideas to life, and boy, did she ever! Carmen is an amazing talent and a tireless worker, and I can't imagine doing this book with anyone but her.

Finally, an apology to my friend Don Wayne (if he's paying attention from the other side) for not thinking to include his wonderful song "Country Bumpkin" in this collection. It just hit me this very day when I thought, "Oh, no! How could I have forgotten that gem?" But we're already past deadline and need to move on.

—Bobby Braddock

ILLUSTRATOR'S NOTES

To quote Kris Kristofferson, "Why me, Lord?" What have I ever done to deserve my fabulous husband, Hap, who kept things running smoothly and encouraged me while I labored over the eighty-one illustrations in this book? And to Bobby Braddock, who came up with a great idea for a different kind of book and chose me to illustrate his vision, I am eternally grateful. Bobby has written many of country's greatest lines himself, although he is too modest to include them in the book. Even though he wrote "I Wanna Talk About Me"—which does have some of country's greatest lines, by the way—he won't talk about himself, so I am doing it for him.

—CARMEN BEECHER

CHAPTER 1

1940s AND 1950s

The silence of a falling star/
Lights up a purple sky

"I'M SO LONESOME I COULD CRY"
Written by Hank Williams
Recorded by Hank Williams for MGM

Hear that lonesome whippoorwill / He sounds too blue to fly / The midnight train is whining low / I'm so lonesome I could cry." Sometimes called "the Hillbilly Shakespeare," homely, skinny Hank Williams burst onto the scene at age twenty-two, and by age twenty-nine he was gone. Country music's first touring singer/writer superstar was, like many of the future country stars, a farm boy from the South who looked like a cowboy from the West. In fact, his band—made up mostly of Alabamians like himself—was called The Drifting Cowboys. So from this 1949 Hank Williams song, this imagery comes to mind: a lonesome cowboy sitting by the campfire, as a distant star, like Hank's star, shoots across the midnight sky and burns out. "The silence of a falling star / Lights up a purple sky / And as I wonder where you are / I'm so lonesome I could cry."

If my wife and I are fussin', brother that's our right/
'Cause me and that sweet woman's got a license to fight

"MIND YOUR OWN BUSINESS"
Written by Hank Williams
Recorded by Hank Williams for MGM

When Hank Williams—country music's substance-abusing superstar of the late 1940s and early 1950s—was a kid in southern Alabama, he learned to play guitar from a black street singer named Tee Tot. You could hear that African American influence whenever Hank wrote an occasional "twelve-bar blues." The first verse of the twelve-bar blues tune "Mind Your Own Business" was right out of the life of Hank and his wife, Audrey. Men and women have been making love and war ever since the world began, and the country songs of Hank Williams's era often became hits when the listening audience identified with his lyrics. So when the line about "if the wife and I are fussin'" started blaring out of mid-twentieth-century car radios, ears started perkin' up throughout small-town and rural America as ol' Hank's words painted a portrait of the listeners' own lives.

Yes, I lost my little darlin' the night they were
playing/
The beautiful Tennessee Waltz

"THE TENNESSEE WALTZ"
Written by Pee Wee King and Redd Stewart
Recorded by Patti Page for Mercury and by many, many others

This song doesn't have any profound lines—in fact, it has just one simple verse and chorus that are then repeated—but all the lines together tell a simple, intriguing story that, along with a beautiful melody, captures a snapshot of a long-ago time and place. When Pee Wee King wrote it in 1946 as an instrumental for his band, the Golden West Cowboys, it was "No Name Waltz." Two years later, Redd Stewart and Pee Wee put words to it, and it became "Tennessee Waltz," which they took to Fred Rose at Acuff-Rose Publishing. From 1948 to 1968, it was on the country charts by Pee Wee King (twice), Cowboy Copas, Roy Acuff and Lacy J. Dalton; in the R&B charts by Erskine Hawkins, Stick McGhee and Johnny Jones; and on the pop charts by Guy Lombardo, Les Paul & Mary Ford, Jo Stafford, Spike Jones, the Fontaine Sisters, Anita O'Day, Bobby Comstock, Jerry Fuller and Sam Cooke. But it was Patti Page, changing the title from "Tennessee Waltz" to "*The* Tennessee Waltz," who brought the song such enduring and endearing fame. Patti's version, featuring her singing harmony with herself, was both a country and pop hit, topping the pop charts for an incredible thirteen weeks and selling 6 million copies. It also became the Tennessee state song and the all-time *biggest-selling* song in Japan.

I take the chance / to lose my
Soul, my life, my pride /
I take the chance /
To be with you

"I TAKE THE CHANCE"
Written by Charlie Louvin and Ira Louvin
Recorded by The Browns for RCA Victor

"I Take the Chance" was written by the Louvin Brothers, Ira and Charlie, the renowned duo whose sweet, perfect harmonies bridged the gap between country and bluegrass. It was recorded by The Browns—Jim Ed, Maxine and Bonnie—another great sibling act who would have their biggest record to date with this song and then, three years later, become world famous for their huge pop-country crossover hit "The Three Bells." "I Take the Chance" was a staple of the country music diet: the cheatin' song. Let's use our imagination and go back to 1956, one day during lunch hour. Two cars are parked in front of a motel room on the edge of town. A pretty young woman in her early twenties, a secretary for a local attorney, emerges from a Chevrolet and walks toward a trim, handsome guy standing by his Oldsmobile, a building contractor a few years older than she is, from a larger city a few counties away. They had met when he hired her boss to represent him in a lawsuit a few months before. He's married, she's single. He tells her he loves her and hopes to marry her someday. He is the love of her life. Then imagine the characters several decades later. He's recently widowed and lives in a nursing home and barely remembers his long-ago girlfriend. In fact, he barely remembers anything. And the long-ago girlfriend's children, grandchildren and great-grandchildren would be shocked and appalled if they knew her secret. She gave up on the building contractor decades ago, married a nice man (now deceased), raised a family and now focuses on her church work and her hobby of making stuffed animals. But sometimes when she falls asleep at night, once again she's a pretty young woman in a tight black sweater and green skirt with crinolines, walking into a motel room with a trim, handsome man wearing dark slacks and a windbreaker jacket. They took the chance—for a memory.

Jambalaya, Crawfish Pie, and Filé Gumbo

"JAMBALAYA (ON THE BAYOU)"
Written by Hank Williams
Recorded by Hank Williams for MGM

When Sony/ATV bought country music publishing giant Acuff-Rose in 2001, two of the greatest assets acquired were Acuff-Rose creative director Troy Tomlinson (who within three years would be heading up the entire Sony publishing organization in Nashville) and the catalog of legendary artist/writer Hank Williams. "Jambalaya," which spent fourteen weeks at #1 on *Billboard*'s country charts in 1952—and made the Top 20 on *Billboard*'s pop charts—was one of the biggest hits of Hank's career. "Jambalaya? Ma cher amio? Thibodaux? Fontaineaux?" Was Hank a world traveler who spent some time in France? No, he was exposed to Cajun French culture—and some of the language—just two states away from his native Alabama, in the swamps of southern Louisiana. This area was settled by French Canadians from the Acadian (hence "Cajun") region in the late eighteenth century. Cajun music, featuring fiddles and accordions and often sung in the original tongue, became a major subgenre of country music. "My Yvonne, the sweetest one, me oh my oh / Son of a gun we'll have big fun on the bayou."

Kaw-Liga was a wooden Indian,/
Standin' by the door,/
He fell in love with an Indian maiden,/
Over in the antique store

"KAW-LIGA"
Written by Hank Williams and Fred Rose
Recorded by Hank Williams, by Charley Pride and by Hank Williams Jr.

Fred Rose came to Nashville from Evansville, Indiana, by way of St. Louis, Chicago, New York's Tin Pan Alley and Hollywood. He and Grand Ole Opry star Roy Acuff founded Acuff-Rose Publishing Company in the early 1940s, and within a few years, their prize songwriter, Hank Williams, was the fastest-rising star in country music. Rose, with songs like "Blue Eyes Crying in the Rain," was a great songwriter himself and often acted as Hank's "song doctor," adding a little polish to the country boy's genius. So when Rose's name actually appeared on the record as co-writer, like this one, you knew that the publisher's contribution was major. "Kaw Liga" (named after a little community in Alabama where Hank owned a fishing cabin) was the only Hank Williams song that was pure fantasy and his only record with a fadeout. "Kaw Liga" spent thirteen weeks at #1; then it flipped over and "Your Cheatin' Heart" was #1 for six weeks, making it a genuine two-sided hit and Hank's biggest record ever. Unfortunately, Hank Williams died of a drug overdose on New Year's Day 1953 and never lived to see the record's success. "Kaw Liga" would also be recorded by Hank Williams Jr. (and by Charley Pride, making it the only hit about a Native American sung by an African American).

Only trouble is, gee whiz/
I'm dreamin' my life away

"ALL I HAVE TO DO IS DREAM"
Written by Boudeleaux Bryant
Recorded by the Everly Brothers for Fraternity

The greatness of this line is that "gee whiz" spoke the language of millions of American teenagers, even though it was written by a thirty-eight-year-old man, Boudeleaux Bryant. The Everly Brothers, hitmakers on both the pop and country charts, became the biggest duo of the early rock 'n' roll era on the strength of songs that Boudeleaux Bryant wrote by himself (such as this one and "Bird Dog") or co-wrote with his wife, Felice (like "Bye Bye Love" and "Wake Up Little Suzie"). They both wrote several solo hits for other artists, and together they wrote the country classic "Rocky Top." Boudeleaux and Felice Bryant are in the Songwriters Hall of Fame, Nashville Songwriters Hall of Fame, Georgia Music Hall of Fame and the Country Music Hall of Fame.

Today I passed you on the street/
And my heart fell at your feet

"I CAN'T HELP IT (IF I'M STILL IN LOVE WITH YOU)"
Written by Hank Williams
Recorded by Hank Williams for MGM

What could hurt more than walking down the street and passing your ex-girlfriend who's oblivious to you as she gushes over the new love at her side? Like so many Hank Williams songs, the words to this one seem palpable, coming from his tortured soul to our ears. That is, until we get to the bridge of the song and realize that even Hank Williams, the greatest of them all, was not perfect and could come up with a clunker once in a blue moon (and I should know about clunkers). When I hear "It's hard to know another's lips will kiss you / And hold you the way I used to do," I can't help but picture this guy with the biggest lips in the world, walking down the street with his new girlfriend dangling from his mouth.

Cradled by two loving arms that I'll die for/ One little kiss then Felina good-bye

"EL PASO"
Written by Marty Robbins
Recorded by Marty Robbins for Columbia

One of the biggest thrills of my life came one winter day in mid-1960s Nashville at the publishing offices of country superstar Marty Robbins. I was a young piano player, auditioning to be in Marty's band. "Well, Bob, you've got the job," said my new boss. Marty Robbins's near-perfect voice lent itself to just about every sub-style on the country music spectrum, from traditional country tear-jerkers to country-pop love songs to rockabilly to the genre he practically invented: gunfighter ballads. One of those gunfighter ballads, "El Paso," was the very biggest of the many big hits he wrote and recorded. This Grammy winner topped the country charts for seven weeks and the pop charts for two. President Eisenhower, a big fan of cowboy fiction and TV westerns, declared it his all-time favorite song. I don't typically quote Wikipedia, but I think "gripping narrative," "haunting harmonies" and "varied Spanish guitar accompaniment by Grady Martin" pretty much nails it. "Out in the West Texas town of El Paso / I fell in love with a Mexican girl / Nighttime would find me in Rosa's Cantina / Music would play and Felina would whirl." There is competition from "a wild young cowboy." The two men shoot it out, the "handsome young stranger lies dead on the floor" and our protagonist rides fast to "the badlands of New Mexico." After some time, he longs so for Felina that he will go back to El Paso because "my love is stronger than my fear of death." To make a long story short, as he approaches the back door of Rosa's Cantina, he sees "the white puff of smoke from a rifle" and feels "the bullet go deep in my chest." "From out of nowhere Felina has found me / Kissing my cheek as she kneels by my side / Cradled by two loving arms that I'll die for / One little kiss and Felina good-bye."

CHAPTER 2

1960s

I turned twenty-one in prison,/ Doin' life without parole

"MAMA TRIED"
Written by Merle Haggard
Recorded by Merle Haggard for Capitol

Merle Haggard was never sentenced to "life without parole," but he did turn twenty-one in prison. Many of Haggard's songs came from his own life. Had he not been a great singer, it's quite possible that he still would have had a major career as a songwriter. Merle was born in 1937 in Bakersfield, in the agriculture-rich Kern River Valley of central California, where his parents had moved three years before as a part of the great "Dust Bowl" migration from small farms in Oklahoma and Texas. "No one could steer me right but Mama tried." Mama's efforts must have paid off, because after getting out of prison Merle Haggard turned his life around, focusing on a career in music. His musical destiny was not in Tennessee but right there in Bakersfield, where his music and that of Buck Owens contributed to the famous Bakersfield Sound: a rawer, twangier country music style than the Nashville musicians were then playing. I was never able to make much of a personal connection with "the Hag," as he was called. One night, I rode around with him and songwriter Dean Dillon for about an hour and a half smoking weed, and I don't think Merle said more than a dozen words. Still waters run deep. "Mama Tried" was the fifth of thirty-eight #1 singles in one of the biggest careers in country music. Merle Haggard died on April 6, 2016, on his seventy-ninth birthday.

They say that time/
Heals a broken heart,/
But time has stood still/
Since we've been apart

"I Can't Stop Loving You"
Written by Don Gibson

*Recorded by Don Gibson for RCA Victor, by Kitty Wells for Decca
and by Ray Charles for ABC Paramount*

In 1957, Don Gibson checked into the York Motel in Nashville and wrote "Oh Lonesome Me" and "I Can't Stop Loving You." He soon recorded both songs for RCA Victor and had a two-sided hit, as well as a major career as a country star for the next fifteen years. Kitty Wells's version of "I Can't Stop Loving You" went to #3 on the country charts. In 1962, Ray Charles, famous for infusing rhythm and blues and rock 'n' roll with soul music from the church, decided to record an album of country songs. Although his recording contract guaranteed him artistic freedom, his record label tried hard to talk him out of it. They need not have worried. *Modern Sounds in Country and Western Music* was America's #1 album for fourteen weeks, and "I Can't Stop Loving You" became the biggest record of Ray Charles's career. The most famous words in the recording were probably not Don Gibson's lines but "brother Ray's" nod to the vocal group: "Sing the song, children."

Hello walls, how'd things go for you today

"HELLO WALLS"
Written by Willie Nelson
Recorded by Faron Young for Capitol

Faron Young, colorful and outspoken, had his first hit in 1953, when he was twenty years old and in the U.S. Army. Eight years later, he had the biggest record of his career, "Hello Walls." It was written by a clean-cut young man (who often wore a suit and tie) named Willie Nelson, a few years before his emergence as a longhaired pot-smoking superstar. This million-seller spent nine weeks at #1 on *Billboard*'s country charts and hit #12 on the pop charts. Nelson's jazzy phrasing strongly influenced Faron Young's performance. In the unique song, the lonely protagonist is carrying on a conversation with the walls, the ceiling and a window. Well-known country deejay Ralph Emery scored a Top 5 hit with the answer to "Hello Walls" ("Hello fool, look around, we're the walls.")

You walk by and I fall to pieces

"I Fall to Pieces"
Written by Hank Cochran and Harlan Howard
Recorded by Patsy Cline for Decca

Shortly after scoring a dual-market smash called "Walkin' After Midnight" in 1957, Patsy Cline was in a serious car accident that almost cost her her life. Then the long recuperation almost cost her her career. But opportunity came knocking again in 1961, when "I Fall to Pieces," written by songwriting giants Hank Cochran and Harlan Howard, soared to the top of the country charts and to #12 on the pop charts. What words could better describe the anguish one feels when running into somebody they love but can't have? "You walk by and I fall to pieces." Two years later, Patsy was in a tragic plane crash, along with Grand Ole Opry stars Cowboy Copas and Hawkshaw Hawkins. Patsy Cline died, but her career didn't. She continued to chart into the 1990s and is recognized as one of the foremost country singers—and torch singers—of the twentieth century.

I'm crazy for crying,
And crazy for trying,
And I'm crazy
For loving you

"Crazy"
Written by Willie Nelson
Recorded by Patsy Cline for Decca

When I hear the classic country-pop torch song "Crazy," my mind goes back to early 1962, when I was at my parents' house in Florida listening to the Grand Ole Opry on the radio, the crowd going wild as Patsy Cline sang her current super hit (the follow-up to "I Fall to Pieces") over and over and over. Almost three years later, after I got married, I was introduced to Ouija, the board game that supposedly contacts spirits. My bride and I would place our hands on a little plastic planchette that scooted around the board from letter to letter, spelling out "messages" from departed souls. I asked Ouija where Willie Nelson got the idea for writing "Crazy." The answer was "Lying in bed in a hotel room staring at the ceiling, saying, 'I'm crazy.'" So the first time I ever had any alone time with Willie, at a Nashville party in 1971, I told him about the Ouija board and asked him if that was really how he got the idea for the song. He looked at me and said, "Hmmmmm" as he rubbed his chin, then nodded and softly said, "Yeahh."

I'm afloat in the middle of a river,
And I can't climb out on either side

"THE OTHER WOMAN"
Written by Don Rollins
Recorded by Ray Price for Columbia

In 1965, country superstar Ray Price returned to his famous traditional Texas shuffle sound of the 1950s with the powerful hit "The Other Woman," written by a young man named Don Rollins who came to Nashville from Phoenix. Although the record was big, when you Google "The Other Woman" you get the Natalie Portman movie. And although the songwriter was having a hot career (he also wrote Price's "I'm Not Crazy Yet" and the George Jones classic "The Race Is On"), when you Google "Don Rollins" you get another writer with the same name who was writing country hits much later, in the 1990s and the twenty-first century. So I'm happy to shine the spotlight on this deserving writer and his song. Like the character in his song, Rollins, too, was torn between his wife and the other woman with whom he had fallen in love. Serious addiction to alcohol only added to his indecision and despair. Don Rollins cut short his promising career one day when he checked into an Atlanta motel and took his own life.

There's a guard and there's a sad old padre,
arm in arm we'll walk at daybreak

"Green, Green Grass of Home"
Written by Curly Putman
Recorded by Porter Wagoner for RCA Victor and Tom Jones for Parrot

When Curly Putman played his publisher this song about a man's joyous visit to his old hometown—a visit that turned out to be just a Death Row last dream—the response was, "Hmmm, I don't know about these down-home songs," but it was agreed that Curly would do a demo on it. Porter Wagoner recorded the song and took it to #4 on the country charts. Then the singing sensation Tom Jones heard and loved a Jerry Lee Lewis version of it and recorded it himself. It was a big hit in both the United Kingdom and the United States and would eventually be covered by hundreds of artists, including Elvis, with versions in every major language. In the mid- and late 1960s, practically no one on the planet had not heard Curly's masterpiece. Not bad for a "down-home" song. When he passed away in 2016, Curly Putman was eulogized with his own words.

Yes they'll all come to see me
In the shade of that old oak tree
When they lay me 'neath the green, green grass of home

Don't open the door to heaven if I can't come in

"DON'T TOUCH ME"
Written by Hank Cochran
Recorded by Jeannie Seely for Monument

Country Music Hall of Fame songwriter Hank Cochran wrote "Don't Touch Me" for his girlfriend, Jeannie Seely, who recorded it and had a big debut hit with it in 1966. (Several other artists recorded it, including country singer Wilma Burgess and jazz legend Ella Fitzgerald.) Hank and Jeannie soon married, and about five years later, I ran into them at a music biz gathering in a large party room at an apartment complex in southeast Nashville. They were bickering, and after a while, I overheard Jeannie snap at Hank, "Don't *touch* me," as life imitated art.

Your love scares me to death, babe,
it's the chokin' kind

"THE CHOKIN' KIND"
Written by Harlan Howard
Recorded by Waylon Jennings for RCA Victor and by Joe Simon for Sound Stage 7

Harlan Howard is generally acknowledged as the all-time greatest country songwriter—the reason his image adorns the front cover of this book. Harlan's "The Chokin' Kind" was a country hit for Waylon Jennings in 1967, and then two years later it was an R&B and pop hit for Joe Simon. Probably nothing makes someone want their freedom more than being in a claustrophobic relationship with a controlling partner. Harlan Howard once told me, "My problem is that I always treated my wives so good that they never wanted me to leave the house." Harlan's wives would probably tell you that he liked to run around and have fun. Then he met Melanie Smith. By this time, Harlan was getting older and was finally ready to settle down. Melanie became wife number five and used her smarts to turn his publishing company into a flourishing moneymaking operation. And Harlan was happy to stay at home with his pretty young wife. Her love wasn't the chokin' kind.

Mary Ann regrets she's unable to see you again/
We're leaving for Europe next week,/
She'll be busy 'til then

"MARY ANN REGRETS"
Written by Harlan Howard
Recorded by Burl Ives for Decca

Burl Ives was a noted actor on Broadway and in Hollywood films, as well as a singer of folk songs and Christmas tunes like "A Holly Jolly Christmas" from the TV classic *Rudolph the Red-Nosed Reindeer*, which he also narrated. In the early 1960s, Ives came to Nashville to record and as a result had some big country and pop hits. My favorite of these is this wonderful Harlan Howard song. I think Carmen Beecher's illustration sums up the song—the rich lady condescendingly writing to the poor boy that he doesn't fit in her Mary Ann's plans. The song gets even sadder, as Mary Ann never gets over her banished boyfriend and dies of a broken heart.

*The only time I wish you weren't gone/
Is once a day, every day, all day long*

"ONCE A DAY"
Written by Bill Anderson
Recorded by Connie Smith for RCA Victor

The country music star who has had the most success as a *songwriter* is Bill Anderson. He not only wrote most of his own hits but also wrote a lot of big ones for other artists. In 1963, he was impressed with a good-looking, big-voiced singer named Connie Smith, whom he saw performing at a theme park near Columbus, Ohio. Bill invited Connie to come to Nashville and record some of his songs for him to pitch to other artists. Chet Atkins at RCA Victor was so impressed when he heard Connie's voice that he signed her to the label. Raised in poverty in West Virginia and Ohio and one of fifteen children, Connie Smith saw all her country dreams come true the first time around. Bill Anderson's super clever "Once a Day" was her first single, released in the summer of 1964. It spent eight weeks at #1 and became one of the biggest debut records of all time. Forty-eight chart records and forty-eight years later, Connie Smith was inducted into the Country Music Hall of Fame.

My eyes look like a road map of Georgia

"SORROW ON THE ROCKS"
Written by Tony Moon
Recorded by Porter Wagoner for RCA Victor

Songwriter, guitarist, producer, arranger Tony Moon was part of the hit band Dante and the Evergreens before leaving his native Los Angeles for Nashville to work with singer Brenda Lee. He'd had a song recorded by the Beatles (and eventually one recorded by Pearl Jam) but also had some successful country songs such as this 1964 Porter Wagoner hit, "Sorrow on the Rocks." Ah, Porter Wagoner. The rhinestone-studded Country Music Hall of Famer was famous for various roles: country chartmaker for decades, star of the most famous of the weekly country music syndicated TV shows, Dolly Parton's mentor and the inspiration for her song "I Will Always Love You." After the passing of Roy Acuff, Porter became the unofficial spokesman-in-chief for the Grand Ole Opry. (If you asked some of the Music Row old-timers to reminisce about Porter Wagoner and tell you what else he had been famous for, you would probably evoke grins from the men and blushes from the ladies.) When I first heard "Sorrow on the Rocks," I thought how perfectly "my eyes look like a roadmap of Georgia" described a guy on a several-day drinking binge. When Carmen Beecher was speculating on how to draw the eyes of this song's protagonist, I suggested that she look at a roadmap of Georgia. She did, and from the looks of this guy's eyes, I think it served her well.

People walkin' up to you
Singin' glory hallelujah
And they try to sock it to you
In the name of the Lord

"GAMES PEOPLE PLAY"
Written by Joe South

Recorded by Joe South for Capitol and Freddy Weller for Columbia

Joe South—Atlanta singer, writer and in-demand session guitarist—wrote and recorded the Grammy-winning pop hit "Games People Play," describing the lifestyles and attitudes of the late 1960s. His friend, another Atlanta guitarist, named Freddy Weller, covered it and had a country hit. South wrote other big ones: "Walk a Mile in My Shoes" and "Don't It Make You Want to Go Home" for himself; "These Are Not My People" for Weller; "Down in the Boondocks" for Billy Joe Royal; "Hush" for Deep Purple; and Lynn Anderson's award-winning crossover monster, "Rose Garden." I got to know Joe in the 1980s, when he was living in Nashville, mostly in party mode and dating local rock 'n' roll queen Marshall Chapman. His contribution to pop and country music was major, and wherever Joe South went, his classic "Games People Play" was never far behind. The "sock it to you in the name of the Lord" line reminds me of a popular faith-healing televangelist.

I'm a man of means
By no means

"KING OF THE ROAD"
Written by Roger Miller
Recorded by Roger Miller for Smash

"Trailers for sale or rent/rooms to let fifty cents" was playing on practically every radio station, both country and pop, in the spring of 1965. Roger Miller had already had two major crossover hits the previous year in "Dang Me" and "Chug a Lug." This one, "King of the Road," would be the five-Grammy-winning monster that showed he was no flash in the pan. This clever writer and singer of both serious and silly songs would soon land his own TV show on NBC. Buddy Killen of Tree Publishing Company (now Sony/ATV) was Roger Miller's publisher, mentor and big brother from the time Roger came to Nashville while still in his teens. Buddy got Roger's songs recorded left and right, saw him blossom as a hit songwriter and then watched him skyrocket to superstardom. Roger's hobo elegy was blasting out of my car radio the day I drove from my little house in South Nashville to Tree Publishing for an appointment with Buddy Killen. I knew that Tree had just surpassed Acuff-Rose (also now Sony/ATV) as Nashville's top music publishing company, and I wanted to write for them. Buddy was enthusiastic about my songs and signed me immediately. He saw me not only as a hit songwriter but also as a singing star, and in interviews he often touted me as "the next Roger Miller." I somehow managed to get five major recording deals over the years, but nothing that I sang ever got higher than #58 on the *Billboard* charts. I was blessed with a songwriting career that exceeded my dreams, but as a recording artist I was, well, no Roger Miller.

They say she took it pretty hard,
but you can't tell too much behind a veil

"Ballad of Forty Dollars"
Written by Tom T. Hall
Recorded by Tom T. Hall for Mercury

No song epitomizes why Tom T. Hall was known as "the storyteller" more than this one. It's about a couple of gravediggers, one who seems to know a little more than the other about the folks who are gathering at the grave site across the way: "Well, that must be the widow in the car and would you take a look at that / That sure is a pretty dress, you know, some women do look good in black." When he says, "They say she took it pretty hard, but you can't tell too much behind a veil," I can just imagine her face up close, not so much grief as relief, almost but not quite smiling, scheming, thinking about all that money and who she's going to spend it with. You continue to hear the voice of perhaps some old boy in 1968 small-town Kentucky: "Well listen, ain't that pretty when the bugler plays the military taps / I think that when you's in the war they always hide 'n' play a song like that." But then we learn that the deceased had run into the gravedigger/narrator just a few days before—probably went off without his billfold—and hit the poor old guy up for a little money. "Well here I am and there they go, and I guess you'd just call it my bad luck / I hope he rests in peace, the trouble is the fellow owes me forty bucks."

When I've learned enough to really live
I'll be old enough to die

"WHEN I'VE LEARNED"
Written by Ray Baker, Buddy Killen and Delbert Whitson
Recorded by Bobby Bare for RCA Victor

Buddy Killen was hired in 1953, when he was twenty years old, to listen to songs for Tree, a brand-new publishing company. By the time I had signed to Tree as a songwriter thirteen years later, Killen had single-handedly turned it into Nashville's top publishing complex and was executive vice-president (and in another fourteen years the sole owner). I soon became aware of a song Buddy had written with songwriter Delbert Whitson and record producer Ray Baker, "When I've Learned." Although the song never became a big hit, it was generally thought of on Music Row as an example of a perfectly written country song. It was recorded by Bobby Bare, an artist widely regarded to be as substantial as the material. "I have met the master on my knees, been tested and been tried / And I've seen God of Heaven paint the fields and countryside / I've been the husband of one wife, heard my newborn baby cry / But when I've learned enough to really live, I'll be old enough to die." I wanted our illustration to show a young man contemplating an aged couple who seemed to be the personification of wealth and happiness as they joyously strolled through the park, maybe old enough to die but still alive and loving every minute of the life they've learned to really live.

It's not her heart lord, it's her mind/
She didn't mean to be unkind/
Why she even woke me up to say goodbye

"SHE EVEN WOKE ME UP TO SAY GOODBYE"
Written by Doug Gilmore and Mickey Newbury
Recorded by Jerry Lee Lewis for Smash

Jerry Lee Lewis was one of the hottest stars in rock 'n' roll in the late 1950s until he married his thirteen-year-old cousin and his career came to a screeching halt. Ten years later, Jerry Lee started singing country and spent more than twenty years on the national charts. This 1969 country hit was written by Doug Gilmore and the legendary writer/artist Mickey Newbury. I came to truly identify with this song years later when someone very special to me started seeing someone else. So many times, eaten up with guilt, she sweetly asked me not to give up on her, reassuring me that she still loved me and that it was just her "crazy mind." More than a few times, I thought, "It's not her heart, Lord, it's her mind, she didn't mean to be unkind." Then one morning, yes, she even woke me up to say goodbye.

CHAPTER 3

1970s

I'll just keep on falling in love 'til I get it right

"'TIL I GET IT RIGHT"
Written by Larry Henley and Red Lane
Recorded by Tammy Wynette for Epic

One day in the early 1970s, I walked into a writers room at Tree International Publishing (now Sony/ATV) on Nashville's Music Row, where master songwriters Larry Henley and Red Lane were working away. I was mesmerized by what I heard. Their melody was moody and jazzy, and the words were powerful. "My door to love has opened out more times than in / And I'm either fool or wise enough to open it again / 'Cause I'll never know what's beyond that mountain 'til I reach the other side / So I'll just keep on falling in love 'til I get it right." Larry asked me what I thought. I said, "I think you guys are writing a great song and I need to get out of your way." The lyric had Tammy Wynette written all over it. (She would have five husbands—including country legend George Jones—and a romantic involvement with movie idol Burt Reynolds.) Tammy cut the song and took it to #1. I was fortunate to have nineteen Tammy Wynette cuts, some of them hits, but nobody ever wrote a Tammy Wynette song as good as "'Til I Get It Right."

Why me, Lord/
What have I ever done/
To deserve even one/
Of the pleasures I've known?

"WHY ME"
Written by Kris Kristofferson
Recorded by Kris Kristofferson for Monument

In the late 1960s, we songwriters at Tree Publishing Company in Nashville would go to Columbia Recording Studios, where we recorded demos of our songs, which would then be pitched to record labels and recording artists. The new janitor at the studios—a tall, good-looking guy named Kris—would lay down his push broom and proceed to pick my brain about songwriting. I soon learned that Kris was four years older than me and had been a Rhodes Scholar at Oxford, a captain in the U.S. Army and a helicopter pilot. He had come to Nashville to start at the bottom and try to realize his music dreams. He wasn't a janitor for long. The songs he wrote would redefine the kinds of songs that came out of Nashville. He also became a successful recording artist and an internationally acclaimed movie star. Whenever I ran into him over the years, he was always the same cheerful, down-to-earth guy with a winning smile and a twinkle in his blue eyes. Kris Kristofferson exemplified that modesty and humility when he recorded the biggest hit of his singing career, asking that famous question in his wonderfully rugged voice, "Why me, Lord?

Yesterday is dead and gone
And tomorrow's out of sight
And it's sad to be alone
Help me make it through the night

"HELP ME MAKE IT THROUGH THE NIGHT"
Written by Kris Kristofferson
Recorded by Sammi Smith for Mega

In the first several months of 1971, it was coming out of radios tuned to both country and pop stations throughout America, the record that started off with the sultry-voiced girl singing "Take the ribbon from my hair / Shake it loose and let it fall." The song was intimate in a way that was unusual for country in those days. The singer, Sammi Smith, had been given the song the year before by that songwriting janitor (Kristofferson) who worked at the studio where she was recording. I met twenty-seven-year-old Sammi when "Help Me Make It..." was a monster hit; I was visiting Ralph Emery at his all-night radio show at WSM in Nashville, and she came in to be interviewed. She brought along her overall-clad daddy from Oklahoma, and I was touched by the way that she seemed just as proud of him as he was of her. Few recording artists ever have a hit this big, but it was the only #1 that Sammi ever had, and she eventually went back to Oklahoma, where she died some years later from emphysema. When "Help Me Make It Through the Night" was released, most of the recent country hits had been about long-term relationships. This one was about a lonely woman in need of a warm body. In my mind, she picked up the phone and called a casual acquaintance and invited him over. "I don't care what's right or wrong / I won't try to understand / Let the devil take tomorrow / But tonight I need a friend."

There's nothing short o' dying/
That's half as lonesome as the sound/
Of the sleeping city sidewalk/
And Sunday morning coming down

"Sunday Morning Coming Down"
Written by Kris Kristofferson

Recorded by Ray Stevens for Monument and by Johnny Cash for Columbia

Another great Kris Kristofferson song. One day in 1969, Kris showed up at Tree Publishing Company, where I was a staff writer. He asked if I wanted to hear a song he had just written, and I said sure. We went into a vacant office, where he sat behind a desk and took his guitar out of its case as I sat across from the desk on a couch. When he finished singing "Sunday Morning Coming Down," he asked, "Well, whadda ya think?" I said, "It's a really good song, but I don't think it's very commercial. I don't know who would record it." Well, Ray Stevens would record it, and so would Johnny Cash. Johnny Cash's version was a very big hit (and I was a very big dummy).

Is anybody going to San Antone,/
Or Phoenix, Arizona,/
Anywhere is all right as long as I/
Can forget I've ever known her

"Is Anybody Going to San Antone"
Written by Dave Kirby and Glenn Martin

Recorded by Charley Pride for RCA Victor

"Is Anybody Going to San Antone" was written by Dave Kirby and Glenn Martin. Kirby was an outrageously funny in-demand guitarist who one night shocked a large gathering at a music-biz meets high society dinner. When it came to his turn, he stood and announced, "My name is Dave Kirby, and I once fucked a bear for the FBI." Glenn Martin sold his Atlanta music store when he was thirty-eight and moved to Nashville and a successful songwriting career. Their 1970 song was the third of Charley Pride's twenty-nine number ones. Pride was an anomaly, an African American country singer, and in a racially conscious 1966 America, RCA Victor released his first record with no publicity about his ethnicity. People were lined up around the block at theaters and auditoriums throughout the southland to hear this hot new singer with the distinctive country twang. There was always a collective gasp from the all-white audience when Charley Pride walked out onstage. But then he'd say, "Bet you weren't expecting to see a fella with a permanent suntan," everybody would laugh and from that moment on he had 'em in the palm of his hand.

There's nothin' cold as/
Ashes after the fire is gone

"AFTER THE FIRE IS GONE"
Written by L.E. White
Recorded by Loretta Lynn and Conway Twitty for Decca

Conway Twitty and Loretta Lynn weren't lovers, and I don't even know if they were good friends before recording together. But they had a great blend, and they were both on the Decca label with the same producer, the great Owen Bradley. Had neither of them had huge solo careers, they would still have been a major recording act as a duo, with ten singles, all of them hits. This one from 1971, written by well-respected traditional writer L.E. White, was their first duet. It spent two weeks at #1 on the country charts and got to #56 on the pop charts. "Love is where you find it / When you find no love at home, And there's nothing cold as ashes / After the fire is gone." That pretty much says it.

While I'm puttin' on my makeup,/
I'm puttin' on the one that really loves me

"THE MIDNIGHT OIL"
Written by Joe Allen
Recorded by Barbara Mandrell for Columbia

Joe Allen and I were bad boys, out partying when we should have been home with our wives and young children. It was one dark night in the early 1970s, and because he was not as messed up as I was, Joe was driving me home. He was a talented songwriter and musician, three-eighths Native American (one parent was one-half, the other one-fourth), and he said there were evil spirits around the interstate exit near my house. Then he got excited because I had just told him God only knows what, and it had given him a song idea. He told me his idea was "When I'm puttin' on my coat and tie, I'm puttin' on the one that really loves me," and asked me to write it with him. It all went over my head, so Joe dropped me off at my house and then went home to write it by himself. Genius producer Billy Sherrill changed "coat and tie" to "my makeup," making it a female song, and recorded it on Barbara Mandrell. It became one of the early hits in her long and successful career. Joe Allen wrote several hits for Gene Watson, including "Should I Go Home (or Should I Go Crazy)," Glen Campbell's "Manhattan Kansas" and Ray Price's "It Don't Hurt Half as Bad."

Mammas don't let your babies grow up to be cowboys/
Don't let 'em pick guitars and drive them old trucks/
Let 'em be doctors and lawyers and such

"Mammas Don't Let Your Babies Grow Up to Be Cowboys"
Written by Ed Bruce and Patsy Bruce
Recorded by Waylon and Willie for RCA and Ed Bruce for United Artists

This song went to #15 on the *Billboard* country charts in 1975 as recorded by Ed Bruce, who wrote it with his wife, Patsy. Two years later, it became an anthem of country music's outlaw movement when Waylon Jennings and Willie Nelson teamed up and topped the charts with it for four weeks and won a Grammy. The outlaw subgenre, epitomized by pot-smoking Willie and tough-talking Waylon, was sort of a protest against the Nashville Sound—that smooth, slick, pop-flavored style of country that had been around since the 1950s. Both men became superstars with their rougher, edgier style of country.

Back when we were young/
Everybody came to see us/
Everybody wanted to be us

"BACK WHEN WE WERE YOUNG"
Written by Tom T. Hall
Recorded by Tom T. Hall for Mercury

Tom T. Hall did very well in Nashville as a songwriter ("Harper Valley P.T.A."), but he did even better as a songwriting artist, scoring several big hits from the late 1960s to the mid-1970s. Well known for his story songs—sometimes sad, often funny, always folksy and clever—he came to be known as "The Storyteller." Actually, "Back When We Were Young" was the B-side of his big crossover hit "I Love," but as I listen to it today, it reminds me of younger party days of wine and weed, songwriters and significant others, thinking we were all so fabulous and fun. Tom T. Hall may have been thinking of himself and his vivacious English-born wife, Dixie, and how "everybody came to see us, everybody wanted to be us."

I got it one piece at a time/
And it didn't cost me a dime

"ONE PIECE AT A TIME"
Written by Wayne Kemp

Recorded by Johnny Cash for Columbia

Although Johnny Cash was one of country music's great singer/songwriters, some of his biggest hits, like "A Boy Named Sue" and "Sunday Morning Coming Down" were outside material. "One Piece at a Time," written by traditional country singer/writer/guitarist Wayne Kemp, was a clever novelty song that was a departure for the writer but probably his biggest hit. It's the tale of a guy on a Detroit assembly line who put together his own custom-built car by sneaking out one part a day in his lunch pail. The song was a country and pop smash in 1976. I had the honor of inducting Wayne into the Nashville Songwriters Hall of Fame in 1999. An unpretentious Arkansas country boy who had a lot of friends, Wayne Kemp died of complications from diabetes in 2015.

Watch how he holds her/
As the band plays/
The last cheater's waltz

"Last Cheater's Waltz"
Written by Sonny Throckmorton
Recorded by T.G. Sheppard for Warner/Curb

"Ooo ooo ooo, don't it sound lonely / Ooo ooo oo, don't they play sad." A roomful of songwriters and their significant others were crowded into the office of Tree Publishing's creative director, Don Gant, one fall night in 1978. They sat in chairs, on the sofa and all over the floor. All of us, male and female alike, were swooning over the beautiful, soulful, high tenor voice of our friend, Sonny Throckmorton, crooning over the big speakers. We were loving the record he had just made. We were so sure that this great songwriter was about to have his shot at stardom. It didn't become a hit for Sonny, but it did for T.G. Sheppard—the biggest record of his big career. When you hear this song, you can feel the hurt of this couple as they dance their farewell dance (and maybe the girl is hurting more because her lover has a wife at home). If you get a chance, hear Sonny Throckmortons's original. Then listen to T.G.'s version. Two great renditions. I can't convey this sad and beautiful melody, but I can share some more of Sonny's poignant words: "He tells her he loves her and the music plays on / He tells her he needs her but there's someone at home / The ball game's all over and she knows she's lost / As the band plays the last cheater's waltz."

While he's kicking his shoes off,
She's putting hers on/
She's got the Friday night blues

"FRIDAY NIGHT BLUES"
Written by Sonny Throckmorton and Rafe Van Hoy
Recorded by John Conlee for MCA

One cool night in the fall of 1978, I was watching various country music acts perform at an outdoor venue somewhere in Nashville during Country Music Week. I had been standing next to a guy whom I knew only as John, a deejay on a local rock station, a personable fellow, nice looking, a little short and stocky. When whoever was singing had finished, John said, "I'll see you later" and headed for the stage, where he was introduced as John Conlee, the singer of the big new hit "Rose Colored Glasses," which was racing up the country charts. It was his first of many hits. Because John's producer, Bud Logan, was affiliated with Tree International Publishing, a lot of us who wrote there would get some John Conlee cuts in the years ahead. Sonny Throckmorton and Rafe Van Hoy got several, and this one, "Friday Night Blues," they wrote together. While Rafe was known for deep lyrics and intricate melodies, Sonny was known for earthy lyrics and melodies that were like Native American chants or haunting cries of despair. The combination of the two songwriting styles was bound to be good. This one has what was once a familiar theme: the husband coming home from a hard day at work, tired and wanting to relax, while the wife is full of energy and ready to go out on the town.

You got to know when to hold 'em,/
Know when to fold 'em

"THE GAMBLER"
Written by Don Schlitz
Recorded by Kenny Rogers for United Artists

Don Schlitz wrote some of the biggest country hits of the 1980s and '90s, many of them with Paul Overstreet, but he wrote his most famous song alone, in 1978, when he was a young man with flowing hair and a long beard. The song was "The Gambler," recorded by country/pop megastar Kenny Rogers. I can think of no other song with as many great lines. Classic opener: "On a warm summer's eve / On a train bound for nowhere / I met up with the gambler / We were both too tired to sleep." Unforgettable chorus: "You got to know when to hold 'em / Know when to fold 'em / Know when to walk away / And know when to run / You never count your money / When you're sittin' at the table / There'll be time enough for countin' / When the dealin's done." Famous last words: "Every hand's a winner / And every hand's a loser / And the best that you can hope for / Is to die in your sleep." And at the death of the gambler, possibly country music's best all-time payoff: "And somewhere in the darkness / The gambler he broke even / But in his final words I found / An ace that I could keep."

If you leave you're gonna leave
a babblin' fool behind

"BREAK MY MIND"
Written by John D. Loudermilk
Recorded by George Hamilton IV for RCA Victor and Vern Gosdin for Elektra

John D. Loudermilk probably wrote more universally recognized songs than any other songwriter working out of Nashville. When it became known that he was terminally ill, a big tribute show was scheduled at the Franklin Theater in Franklin, Tennessee. It was to be filmed for a PBS special, and the album would be recorded live for release on the Columbia Red label. I was one of about twenty-five who were to perform—most of them were much more famous than me. I told old friend Dixie Gamble, who was producing the show, that I wanted to sing one of my Loudermilk favorites, "Break My Mind," which had been a hit for George Hamilton IV in 1967 and Vern Gosdin in 1978. I had seen Loudermilk do it many times over the years, and whenever he got to the chorus, he would pretend to go totally berserk onstage and it was greatly entertaining. On the chilly March 2016 night of the tribute, I came on somewhere in the middle of the show. It had been a wonderful evening, with a joyous John D. in attendance, seated at the front of the theater. After a brief shout-out to the honoree, I broke into "Break My Mind." When I got to the "babblin fool" line, I kept playing piano with my left hand and started flubbering my lips with my right index finger like I'd lost my mind. John D. got a big kick out of it. I wanted him to know I was paying tribute not only to the song but also to the great man who wrote it.

Make up your mind or I'll lose mine

"SHOULD I COME HOME (OR SHOULD I GO CRAZY)"
Written by Joe Allen
Recorded by Gene Watson for Capitol

With a voice naturally tinged with sadness and absent of gimmicks and gymnastics, Gene Watson is possibly one of the most underrated singers in country music. Many of his hits, like "Love in the Hot Afternoon" and "Fourteen Carat Mind," are well known and hold up over the years. When people cite "He Stopped Loving Her Today," which I wrote with Curly Putman, as country music's best dying song, I often point to Lawton Williams's "Farewell Party," as recorded by Gene Watson. And this Joe Allen powerhouse, which was a hit for Gene Watson in 1979, is one of country music's best going-crazy songs. "Last night when I came by, I rang the bell and no one answered / But I heard voices whisper through the door / Now I'm not sure if anyone was home to do the talking / 'Cause lately I hear voices more and more."

CHAPTER 4

1980s

When you try to put love back together,/
There's always a few little pieces you can't find

"TOO MANY RIVERS"
Written by Harlan Howard

Recorded by Brenda Lee for Decca and the Forrester Sisters for Warner

I wrote this about Harlan Howard in my book, *Bobby Braddock: A Life on Nashville's Music Row*: "I think Harlan loved life more than anyone I ever knew. Though named after his ancestral home of Harlan County, Kentucky, he was born in Detroit and brought up in an orphanage there, and he had that Detroit accent (saying 'God dammit' like 'Gyod dimmit')." Generally considered the dean of country songwriters and, in his later years, Music Row's elder statesman, Harlan is credited with coining the expression "three chords and the truth" to describe traditional country music. He went all out with "Too Many Rivers," as it had four chords and the truth. It was a pop hit for Brenda Lee in 1965 and a country hit for the Forrester Sisters in 1987. Harlan's great line tells the truth about those long-lost elements that can never be found when attempting to resurrect an old romance. Like the missing pieces of a puzzle.

She's been walked on and stepped on so many times,/
And I hate to admit it but that last footprint's mine

"LIFE TURNED HER THAT WAY"
Written by Harlan Howard
Recorded by Mel Tillis for Kapp, Ricky Van Shelton for Columbia

Harlan Howard, who was often called the "Irving Berlin of country music," wrote #1 country hits in five consecutive decades, from the 1950s to the 1990s. This song went to #11 on the Billboard country charts with Mel Tillis in 1967 and then to #1 with Ricky Van Shelton in 1988. From the attention-getting opener, "If she seems cold and bitter I beg of you / Just stop and consider all she's gone through," to the payoff in the hook, "So don't blame her, life turned her that way," this is classic country at its best.

*I don't know a thing about love/
I just kind of hang here above*

"I DON'T KNOW A THING ABOUT LOVE" (THE MOON SONG)
Written by Harlan Howard
Recorded by Conway Twitty for Warner

Who else but the legendary Harlan Howard could write a song in the first-person voice of the man in the moon and make a hit out of it? For almost two decades, Conway Twitty had more #1 country hits than any previous artist at that time at thirty-nine. This was his thirty-sixth #1, and my very favorite. Most good songs make a connection with topics that are a part of everyone's consciousness, and I think at some point every kid in the world notices that the moon has a face. My illustrator and I were both born and raised in Polk County, Florida, then America's leading citrus-producing county. We've tried to keep these "song pictures" in the same era as the popularity of the corresponding song, in this case 1984. In that year, you could still find plenty of rural and idyllic spots in Polk County, such as the one pictured here. But today that area, lying midway between Orlando and Tampa, is turning into one big suburbia to both cities—sometimes called "Orlampa"—and you may have to drive around for a while before finding a spot like the one shown here, with no housing developments or condos in sight. But no matter how crowded it gets down here on Earth, that same old man in the moon will still be hanging there above, perhaps telling us that he doesn't know a thing about love.

I wish I was eighteen again/
And going where I've never been

"I WISH I WAS EIGHTEEN AGAIN"
Written by Sonny Throckmorton
Recorded by Jerry Lee Lewis for Elektra and by George Burns for Mercury

In 1980, at the age of eighty-three, George Burns, who had experienced practically every other aspect of show business, became the oldest person in history to debut on the country (and pop) music charts, singing this charming Sonny Throckmorton song. George and Sonny became friends, and whenever the legendary comedian made the rounds on the TV talk show circuit, he always acknowledged Sonny before doing this song. Sonny had a simple but profound approach to songwriting that set him apart, such as rhyming, and comparing, "old folks and old oaks," as he did here. "Eighteen" was also recorded by Jerry Lee Lewis, who hit with Throckmorton's "Middle Age Crazy" in 1977.

I may never get to heaven,/
But I once came mighty close

"I MAY NEVER GET TO HEAVEN"
Written by Bill Anderson and Buddy Killen
Recorded by Conway Twitty for MCA

Conway Twitty is in both the Rockabilly Hall of Fame and the Country Music Hall of Fame. After a successful career as a rock 'n' roller, he became one of the all-time biggest stars in country music. Among his many country hits was this powerful ballad, written by publishing mogul Buddy Killen and country legend Bill Anderson. In 1987, Conway Twitty married Dee Henry. Whenever you saw them together, they would be holding hands, a couple of lovebirds. All these twenty-seven years after Conway's untimely death, this very attractive woman has not even dated anyone, remaining faithful to the memory of the love of her life. A big thanks to Dee for sending us photos from her private collection so we could find an ideal pose of her and Conway together to base our picture on.

Don't you ever get tired of hurting me

"DON'T YOU EVER GET TIRED OF HURTING ME"
Written by Hank Cochran
Recorded by Ray Price for Columbia and Ronnie Milsap for RCA

They say what doesn't kill you makes you stronger. When Hank Cochran was two years old, he contracted pneumonia, whooping cough, measles and mumps all at the same time. The doctor said he would never survive it, but he did. His parents divorced when he was nine, and he was placed in an orphanage (that he ran away from several times). He left his native Mississippi and hitchhiked all around the country as a teenager, working in oil fields in New Mexico and picking olives in California, eventually ending up in Nashville in his early twenties, where he found his niche as a songwriter—what would be a twenty-five-year career of one hit song after the other. Being on his own at an early age may have contributed to his reputation as a great hustler. My favorite Hank Cochran story is the one about him being at a Ray Price recording session, and when the great country crooner went into the control room to talk to his producer, Hank went around the room and taught one of his songs to the musicians. After going back out into the studio, Ray Price told his producer, "Let's do this Hank Cochran song, since the pickers already know it." It may have been this one, "Don't You Ever Get Tired of Hurting Me," which went to #11 in 1966. It went to #11 again years later when Ray recorded it as a duet with Willie Nelson, and then in 1988 it finally went to #1 with Ronnie Milsap. The song is about being in love with someone who doesn't love you back but plays you along—only slightly less painful than having your body stretched on a medieval torture rack.

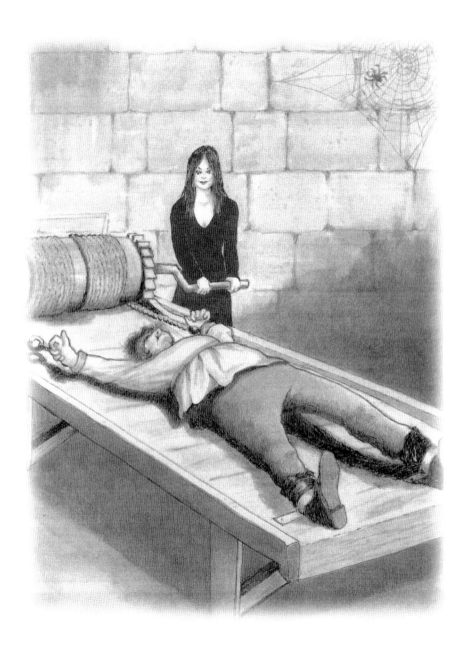

If love never lasts forever
Tell me, what's forever for

"WHAT'S FOREVER FOR"
Written by Rafe Van Hoy
Recorded by Michael Martin Murphey for Liberty

Many, many years ago, in the late evenings, hordes of songwriters would gravitate to the second floor of Nashville's Tree International Publishing. They would crowd into the office of the vice-president in charge of creative, Don Gant, where they would share one another's wine and weed and hear one another's latest songs. One evening, I was in the lobby as songwriter Rafe Van Hoy stepped off the elevator. He told me he had written a new song but wasn't sure if it was good enough to play for the group down the hall in Gant's office. "Why don't you run it by me first?" I asked. We went into a vacant office, where he sang me a song about a "perfect couple" he knew who had surprised everyone by splitting up. I suggested to my friend that he go sing this powerhouse for the group. Michael Martin Murphey, famous for his folk/pop hit of 1975 "Wildfire," would take Rafe's song to the top of the country charts and to #19 on *Billboard*'s pop charts in the fall of 1982. Rafe, the "boy wonder," was married to beautiful singer/writer Deborah Allen (who would soon have a big country/pop crossover hit called "Baby I Lied"). We all thought Rafe and Deborah would last forever, but they didn't. Both went on to other happy marriages. But I wonder, how many of the millions who experienced matrimonial failure have heard this great song over the years and recalled a marriage that began with hope and happiness and then ended with the emptying of a house and two moving vans driving off in opposite directions. "So what's the glory in living / Doesn't anybody ever stay together anymore / And if love never lasts forever / Tell me, what's forever for?"

I'd love to watch you leaving/
Like a hundred times before/
At least my eyes could watch you walk away

"I WISH THAT I COULD HURT THAT WAY AGAIN"
Written by Don Cook, Curly Putman and Rafe Van Hoy
Recorded by T. Graham Brown for Capitol

When you put one of the cleverest writers in Nashville (Don Cook), a musical genius (Rafe Van Hoy) and a legendary writer of sad songs (Curly Putman) together in a room with their guitars, you might expect something at least pretty good and maybe a masterpiece. This one is a masterpiece. Few songs have such potent writing throughout: "At least I had you every now and then," "Your coming back was always worth the pain" and especially this one: "And in between the sorrow / At least there was tomorrow / And as long as there's tomorrow there's no end." Question: What's worse than someone constantly breaking your heart? Answer: Missing that person so much that you would gladly have her (or him) back in your life, breaking your heart. It seems like practically every artist who was pitched this song recorded it: Kenny Rogers, Brenda Lee, John Conlee, Millie Jackson, T.G. Sheppard, David Frizzell, Julie Andrews, T. Graham Brown and many more. In 1986, fully eight years after the song was written, country blues belter T. Graham Brown's version was released as a single and became a big hit.

*When they ask about you and me/
I tell it like it used to be*

"I Tell It Like It Used to Be"
Written by Michael Garvin, Ron Hellard and Bucky Jones
Recorded by T. Graham Brown for Capitol

Before he was a country music star, T. Graham Brown was an in-demand demo singer on Nashville's Music Row. He was often being the first one to hear a new song as it rolled off the assembly line, and in 1985, when it came time for him to get songs to record himself, Brown knew right where to go. The Georgia-born soulful singer remembered a song he had demoed at Tree International Publishing (now Sony/ATV) called "I Tell It Like It Used to Be." The pounding rockaballad was written by Ron Hellard, Bucky Jones and Michael Garvin. Record producers often called this publishing giant and told one of the songpluggers, "I want to hear some songs by 'those three guys at Tree.'" The truth was that "those three guys" were actually five guys who wrote interchangeably in groups of three, the five being Hellard, Jones and Garvin plus two other successful songwriters (and record producers), Tom Shapiro and Chris Waters. (All five of these songwriters have written other hits within this group and with other writers.) Ron Hellard, the funny guy of the group, once cracked up legendary artist/writer Roger Miller with this line: "A lot of folks think me and my co-writers are the next you."

Let me watch my children grow/
To see what they become/
Oh Lord don't let that cold wind blow/
Till I'm too old to die young

"TILL I'M TOO OLD TO DIE YOUNG"
Written by Scott Dooley, John Hadley and Kevin Welch
Recorded by Moe Bandy for Columbia

Male wolves are generally monogamous and stay with their pack, getting to see their pups grow up. That's the prayer of the protagonist in this powerful song, that he be allowed to watch his children grow to see what they become. I can't hear "Till I'm Too Old to Die Young" without thinking of Don Gant, beloved singer, producer and publisher on Nashville's Music Row. He served as Tree International's vice-president and creative director for more than five years before starting his own publishing company, Old Friends, in 1981, where he signed several talented songwriters, including future Brooks & Dunn duo partner Kix Brooks. While at Tree, he was part of our little crowd and became one of my closest friends. But Gant had more close friends than anyone I've ever known and probably mentored hundreds of songwriters. On a windy evening in March 1987, a blood clot from a broken leg caused a massive stroke, and our friend Gant died at age forty-four. He died young. Later that night, at the Bluebird Café, handsome and popular singer/writer Kevin Welch stepped up to the mic and said, "I want to dedicate this to the memory of Don Gant" and then sang the song he had written with John Hadley and Scott Dooley: Moe Bandy's current hit, "Till I'm Too Old to Die Young." "If life is like a candle bright / Death must be the wind / You can close your window tight / And it still comes blowing in."

You won't break my heart, and I don't love you: famous last words of a fool

"FAMOUS LAST WORDS OF A FOOL"
Written by Dean Dillon and Rex Huston
Recorded by George Strait for MCA

On April 9, 1988, George Strait hit #1 on the *Billboard* country chart with "Famous Last Words of a Fool," written by Dean Dillon and Rex Huston. Other George Strait hits written or co-written by Dean Dillon included "Unwound" (1981), "Down and Out" (1981), "Marina Del Rey" (1982), "The Chair" (1985), "Nobody in His Right Mind Would Have Left Her" (1986), "It Ain't Cool to Be Crazy About You" (1986), "Ocean Front Property" (1987), "I've Come to Expect It from You" (1990), "If I Know Me" (1991), "Easy Come, Easy Go" (1993), "Lead On" (1995), "The Best Day" (2000), "She Let Herself Go" (2005), "Living for the Night" (2009), "The Breath You Take" (2010) and "Here for a Good Time" (2011).

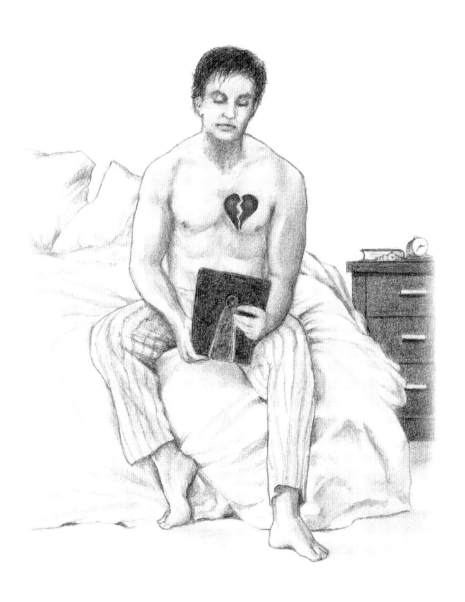

All my exes live in Texas

"ALL MY EXES LIVE IN TEXAS"
Written by Whitey Shafer and Lyndia Shafer
Recorded by George Strait for MCA

Written by ace songwriter Whitey Shafer and his then-wife, Lyndia, this 1987 hit has one of the cleverest titles ever and tells the story of "Rosanna down in Texarkana," "sweet Eileen in Abilene," "Allison in Galveston" and how "Dimples who now lives in Temple's got the law looking for me." Done up in pure western swing style, this was the eleventh #1 for George Strait, who would have more top hits than any artist in country music—forty-four of them. A native Texan like Strait, Whitey Shafer was not only one of country music's most beloved songwriters but also one of its most colorful characters. Like singer Mel Tillis, Whitey had a stutter that he used to comedic effect. In recalling the story of hauling a piano on a flatbed truck through downtown Fort Worth, he told about waiting for a long time at an intersection and how, when the light finally changed to green, he momentarily forgot about the piano and impatiently hit the accelerator hard, sending the big instrument crashing onto the street. Asked if it made a pretty deafening noise, he said, with a twinkle in his eye, "Yeah, but for just a m-m-moment it was a…s-s-s-symphony." Despite all his songs about breakups and exes, he and his last wife, Tracy, had a happy nineteen-year marriage. Sanger D. Shafer passed away on January 12, 2019. I think Whitey would have enjoyed seeing himself "playing the part" of one of his song characters in the mockup newspaper story on the opposite page.

Nashville Banner

Nashville's Newspaper since 1876 • www.NashvilleBanner.com

4 TEXAS WOMEN FILE CLASS-ACTION
LAWSUIT AGAINST LOCAL MAN

Won't wage PTL fight, says Bakker

Denies accusations

May Day protests

Hangs his hat in Tennessee

Their ex-husband

Four female residents of Texas, Rosanna R. Danna of Texarkana, Eileen Wright of Abilene, Allison Keane of Galveston, and Dimples Doolittle of Temple have filed a class action lawsuit against a local man for alienation of affection, back alimony, and general disagreeableness. Additionally, Allison Keane claimed she had experienced extreme emotional and mental distress, which led to a psychotic episode and months of therapy. Dimples Doolittle filed a criminal complaint alleging missing funds and embezzlement. The women met purely by coincidence at a support group called KALE, "Karma and a Lousy Ex."

Comparing notes, they soon found that they were duped by the same man. They joined forces to engage a lawyer and filed the ensuing class action lawsuit.

It is believed that there may be more Texas women who have been duped by the philanderer. Anyone having knowledge of this may contact the firm of Tortsarus, Tortsarus, Howe and Wynn in Austin, Texas. In the words of Rosanna Danna of Texarkana, "As my dad daddy used to say, you can't trust a man who claims his wedding ring has gotten too small." Rosanna believes she was the first wife, but investigations are researching records to be sure.

If you have had a similar experience with a cheating, unfaithful, slick talking con man, contact Karma and a Lousy Ex (KALE) to find wonderful support and good advice on finding a very slick lawyer who will help you seek revenge. Just Google KALE Support Group.

Current wife reacts

Ford vows to speak about case

Says judge's gag order violates Constitution

Regional Mass Transit System called crucial

Quick $4 million for Gore not a certainty

*I don't care what's in your past/
You're as far as I can see*

"THAT'S ALL THAT MATTERS"
Written by Hank Cochran
Recorded by Mickey Gilley for Epic

When Hank Cochran got this song recorded by Ray Price in 1964, it became the B-side of Price's hit "Burning Memories." Sometimes songwriters have to be patient. Sixteen years later, in 1980, it became a #1 hit for singer/pianist/ night club owner Mickey Gilley. Gilley is a first cousin to both country rocker Jerry Lee Lewis and televangelist Jimmy Swaggart. This is a great country love song. "I know other lips have kissed you / I know you've been thrilled and pleased / But mine are the lips that kiss you now / And that's all that matters to me." Perhaps the best thing one can say to a significant other, besides "I love you," is "I will not judge you."

An avalanche of romance,/
A landslide of love

"AVALANCHE OF ROMANCE"
Written by Bobby Braddock and Rafe Van Hoy
Recorded by Bobby Braddock for RCA

When told about this project, several people said that since I had written a lot of country hits, this book should include my songs. I said no, that to name a book *Country Music's Greatest Lines* and then include my own songs would be immodest and embarrassing. But then I thought of one that I *could* include, simply because it's so bad that no one would take me seriously. Actually, Rafe Van Hoy and I set out one night in the late 1970s to write the worst song in the world. The song ended up on my 1983 RCA album *Hardpore Cornography*. My favorite dumb line, besides the title line, is "Your love's like a crevice and I'm falling in." Here's the chorus: "An avalanche of romance, a landslide of love / We got off our big rocks with one little shove / An earthquake for God's sake, a hurricane of heartaches / An avalanche of romance, a landslide of love." There was a country comedy duo in the 1950s and '60s called Lonzo and Oscar, and what they wore could be described as hillbilly clown clothes. I showed Carmen Beecher some pictures of Rafe and me from that era, and asked her to go to the drawing board and dress us up like Lonzo and Oscar, which she did.

You were the first thing that I thought of/
When I thought I drank you off my mind

"KILLIN' TIME"
Written by Clint Black and Hayden Nicholas
Recorded by Clint Black for RCA

A song's most powerful line usually comes in the middle or toward the end of a song, but this one hits you at the very beginning. Clint Black wrote this with his frequent writing partner, Hayden Nicholas. Black, a New Jersey–born, Texas-raised "hat act," burst onto the scene in February 1989, hitting #1 with his first single, "A Better Man," and following up with this one, his second #1 in a long string of hits. Clint's a man who knows what he wants. When I played a writers show with him in 1997, he wanted me to accompany him on "Put Yourself in My Shoes" and was determined to figure out how to tune my keyboard to his harmonica, calling three music stores until he found someone who could tell us how to do it. A first-rate country singer, crackerjack songwriter (he's never had a hit that he didn't write or co-write) and handsome dude who could pass for Roy Rogers's grandson, his success is not surprising. This song will always be remembered for its solid chorus of "This killin' time is killin' me" and its attention-getting opener, which was a brand-new way of saying what Hank Williams had conveyed thirty-six years before: "I can't escape from you."

CHAPTER 5

1990s

Roll the stone away/
Let the guilty pay/
It's Independence Day

"INDEPENDENCE DAY"
Written by Gretchen Peters
Recorded by Martina McBride for RCA

New York–born and Colorado-raised, songwriter Gretchen Peters came to Nashville in the late 1980s. Her big break was also Martina McBride's big break, when the dynamic young singer from Kansas carried "My Baby Loves Me (Just the Way that I Am") to the *Billboard* country Top 5 in 1993. A year later, Martina recorded another Gretchen song, "Independence Day," earning the songwriter a CMA Song of the Year award. It became sort of a rallying cry for battered women. The song's protagonist recalls coming home from the county fair at eight years old to learn that her abused mom has burned their house down while wife-beater Dad was passed out drunk in bed. The child is taken to a county home and, as an adult, reflects, "Now I ain't sayin' it's right or it's wrong, but maybe it's the only way." Ironically, Fox News commentator Sean Hannity heard it as a patriotic song, and during the Iraq War, he played the chorus as his radio talk show theme song: "Let freedom ring / Let the white dove sing, / Let the whole world know that today is a day of reckoning."

You don't even know who I am,/
So what do you care if I go

"YOU DON'T EVEN KNOW WHO I AM"
Written by Gretchen Peters
Recorded by Patty Loveless for Epic

One of country music's best singers, Patty Loveless recorded this song, written by one of country music's best writers, Gretchen Peters, and took it to #5 on the *Billboard* country charts in the spring of 1995. I love the way this song is crafted, how it pulls you in, line by line (in three-quarter time) as a poignant story unfolds.

She left the car in the driveway, she left the key in the door
She left the kids at her mama's, and the laundry piled up on the floor
She left her ring on the pillow, right where it wouldn't be missed
She left a note in the kitchen, next to the grocery list
It said:
You don't even know who I am
You left me a long time ago
You don't even know who I am
So what do you care if I go
He left the ring on the pillow, he left the clothes on the floor
And he called her to say he was sorry, but he couldn't remember what for
So he said I've been doing some thinking, thinking that maybe you're right
I go to work every morning, and I come home to you every night
And you don't even know who I am
You left me a long time ago
You don't even know who I am
So what do I care if you go

With a broken wing
She carries her dreams/
Man you oughta see her fly

"A Broken Wing"
Written by James House, Phil Barnhart and Sam Hogin
Recorded by Martina McBride for RCA

There are a lot of good singers and a considerable number of great ones, but very few have what I call magic (in the voice). Linda Ronstadt had it, and I think Martina McBride has it too. Sounding intimate on the low notes and emotion-packed when belting out the stunning high ones, there's no better example than this two-octave hit from 1997. Adding fuel to the fire is the powerful production (by Paul Worley and Ed Seay) and a vocal backup group that sounds like it could be a choir from maybe the biggest AME Zion Church in Nashville. James House, Phil Barnhart and the late Sam Hogin wrote a song about a woman in an emotionally abusive marriage, subjected to having her dreams constantly shot down by a man who would say, "You're crazy for believing you'll ever leave the ground, only angels know how to fly." Then, one Sunday morning, she didn't go to church, and he wondered why she hadn't left. "He went up to the bedroom / Found a note by the window / With a curtain blowin' in the breeze." The writers intentionally left the ending ambiguous—did she actually leap to her death, or is the broken wing just a metaphor for hobbling away and getting on with her life? "Man you oughta see her fly."

You've got to tend to what you've planted/
And if you take my love for granted/
Baby, I'll shake the sugar tree

"SHAKE THE SUGAR TREE"
Written by Chapin Hartford
Recorded by Pam Tillis for Arista

If asked to give a description of a typical hot new country songwriter in the summer of 1992, those in the know might have said "some guy about twenty-eight years old from a small southern town" or maybe "some young man from Texas." But the writer of this hit, bursting forth on the scene as the writer of Diamond Rio's debut smash "Meet in the Middle" the year before, was a lady from New England in her late forties named Chapin Hartford. Anyone who ran into pretty, petite, hardworking Chapin, totin' her guitar case down the halls of Sony/Tree Publishing in those days, knew that she meant business. Pam Tillis's producers, Paul Worley and Ed Seay, liked the original demo of "Shake the Sugar Tree" so well that they wanted to use the demo tracks for Pam's record, so Chapin not only got royalties as a songwriter but also shared in the production credits. Pam, the Florida-born daughter of legendary Mel Tillis, recorded this unique song when she was eight years into her sixteen-year tenure on the *Billboard* country charts.

*I'm a walkin', talkin', cryin',/
Barely beatin' broken heart*

"WALKIN', TALKIN', CRYIN', BARELY BEATIN' BROKEN HEART"
Written by Roger Miller and Justin Tubb
Recorded by Highway 101 for Warner Brothers

This is one of country music's longer song titles and encompasses most of the last line of each verse. Before Roger Miller's superstar career had taken off, he co-wrote this song with the legendary Ernest Tubb's son Justin, who had already gained attention as a singing heartthrob. The song had been moderately successful for Johnny Wright (Kitty Wells's husband) in 1964 and then a hit in 1990 by Highway 101, a country music band founded in California by Paulette Carlson (lead vocalist), Jack Daniels, Curtis Stone and Scott "Cactus" Moser. I'm afraid it's going to take more than aspirin, nitroglycerin, statins and bypass surgery to save this heart.

Dreams weren't meant to come true,/
That's why they call 'em dreams

"Beautiful Fool"
Written by Don Henry
Recorded by Don Henry for Sony and by Kathy Mattea for Mercury

Don Henry is a genius, a word I take seriously and use sparingly. Don chooses his co-writers carefully and has co-written great songs such as Kathy Mattea's Grammy-winning "Where've You Been" and the more recent Miranda Lambert hit "All Kinds of Kinds." He has also written many great songs by himself, some of them brilliantly funny but some of them dead serious, like this story of Martin Luther King Jr.'s idealistic heroism: "Beautiful Fool." In this autobiographical journey, we witness history through the eyes of an eight-year-old white boy: "Walter Cronkite preempted Disney one night / And all us kids were so upset. / We thought you were a trouble instigator / Marching through our TV set." I highly recommend that you seek out this song, whether Don Henry's original or Kathy Mattea's cover. "Oh you beautiful fool / Swimming upstream and kicking up waves." A beautiful lesson in history. "To fight a fight without a fist / All human instinct puzzles this / How dare you threaten our existence / Mahatma Gandhi, Jesus Christ / History repeats itself so nice / Consistently we are resistant / To love." A beautiful lesson in nonviolence…and love.

Don't tell me what to do/
I'll love you forever if I want to

"DON'T TELL ME WHAT TO DO"
Written by Max D. Barnes and Harlan Howard
Recorded by Pam Tillis for Arista

Harlan Howard's co-writer on this Pam Tillis hit, Max D. Barnes, was similar to Harlan in that he had worked a lot of blue-collar jobs before getting into the music business. However, Max D. (as everyone called him) got into the business a little later in life than most writers. He received his first BMI Award at age forty-two and his CMA Song of the Year award for the classic "Chiseled in Stone" at fifty-three. But Max D. made up for lost time, his name appearing on one big hit after another, many of them standards—he had no fewer than forty-seven songs recorded by Vern Gosdin. I think Max D.'s many years as a blue-collar worker in the Rust Belt gave him a keen insight into the lives of everyday people and a sweet humility that made him stand out in the songwriting community. Max D. Barnes passed away in 2004, two years after Harlan Howard. This song always made me think of some old lady, still clinging to her picture of some long-ago young man, loving him forever if she wants to. Just for fun, we show her holding a picture of a young Harlan, who broke quite a few hearts in his day.

You know your daddy told me when I left/
Jesus would forgive, but a daddy don't forget

"LITTLE ROCK"
Written by Tom Douglas
Recorded by Collin Raye for Epic

We have featured Tom Douglas songs like "Southern Voice" and "Back There Again." This is the story of his very first hit. After graduating from college and working at a few jobs, Tom decided to follow his dream and came to Nashville from his hometown of Atlanta in the late 1970s, staying for four years without much luck. As he put it, he burned his songwriter's clothes and moved to Dallas, where he pursued a career in real estate. In 1993, never able to get the songwriting dream out of his head, he went to a songwriting symposium in Austin, where he got up the nerve to hand a cassette of songs to successful producer/music executive Paul Worley, with whom he had become acquainted in his Nashville days. Worley later called Tom and told him that he liked one of the songs and was going to record it on Collin Raye. He was moved by the power of the melody and the words of "Little Rock": "I think I'm on a roll here in Little Rock." The song was about a recovering alcoholic, telling his wife that he was doing much better and was selling VCRs in Arkansas at a Walmart. "I haven't had a drink in nineteen days / My eyes are clear and bright without that haze / I like the preacher from the Church of Christ / Sorry that I cried when I talked to you last night." The Collin Raye record was a hit. Tom Douglas moved his family to Nashville and became one of country music's most successful and respected songwriters. "The House that Built Me," which he co-wrote, won both the CMA and ACM Song of the Year awards, and in 2014, he was inducted into the Nashville Songwriters Hall of Fame.

Sweeten my coffee with a morning kiss

"THEN YOU CAN TELL ME GOODBYE"
Written by John D. Loudermilk
Recorded by the Casinos, by Eddy Arnold, by Glen Campbell and by Neal McCoy

"Tell me you love me for a million years / Then if it don't work out / If it don't work out / Then you can tell me goodbye." With unique lyrics and a dreamy melody, this, one of America's favorite love songs, was a hit by four different artists in various genres—spanning the 1960s through the 1990s—and was written by John D. Loudermilk. When I first met John D. at a party, he was wearing a suit and standing on his head doing yoga. He enjoyed chasing hurricanes for songwriting energy. His political and religious views could change without warning, and you never knew if his next hit would be pop, rock or country, because he wrote it all. Carmen Beecher did this wonderful sketch from a long-ago photo of John D. and Susan, his best friend, co-conspirator and loving wife from 1971 until the day he died in 2016.

It's all right to be little bitty

"LITTLE BITTY"
Written by Tom T. Hall
Recorded by Alan Jackson for Arista Nashville

In 1996, a number of years after Tom T. Hall had enjoyed his last big hit, Alan Jackson heard "Little Bitty" on Tom T.'s album *Songs from Sopchoppy*, gave it the Jackson touch and took it to the top of the charts. About ten years after that, my friend Shannon McCombs was producing an EPK (electronic press kit) to promote my new book, and about a half dozen country music stars agreed to come by Sony/ATV Publishing to be filmed saying a few kind words. Little Jimmy Dickens and Brenda Lee, coincidentally, showed up at the same time. As I proudly stood between these two legends, though I was much taller than both of them, I never felt that I was looking down at them. When you're a *giant* in the music business like Little Jimmy or Brenda, it's definitely all right to be little bitty.

It's my belief/
Pride is the chief cause/
In the decline in the number/
Of husbands and wives

"HUSBANDS AND WIVES"
Written by Roger Miller
Recorded by Roger Miller for Smash, Brooks & Dunn for Arista Nashville

The great artist/writer Roger Miller not only knew how to write a good song, but he also knew when to stop writing it. "Husbands and Wives" said so much in just one verse and a short bridge that Roger didn't write any more than that—when he recorded it, he simply sang the verse twice and faded out. Roger's record went to #5 on the country charts and #26 on the pop charts in 1966. Thirty-two years later, Brooks & Dunn took it to #1 on the country charts and #36 on the pop charts. A few years before the Brooks & Dunn hit, my good friend Don Cook had taken Kix Brooks, a prolific songwriter in our circle of friends, to Tim DuBois at Arista Records to see if Arista would sign him as an artist. Tim said he was considering signing a guy named Ronnie Dunn and suggested that Don record Kix and Ronnie together as a duo. When they were trying to figure out what to call the new team, I suggested the Coyote Brothers, which Ronnie liked, so they included it on a list of names to consider. Brooks & Dunn went on to become the biggest-selling duo of all time, outselling even giant pop acts like the Everly Brothers and Simon & Garfunkel. I've often wondered if the Coyote Brothers would have been as huge as Brooks & Dunn.

CHAPTER 6

TWENTY-FIRST CENTURY

Tom Petty rocked it/
Dr. King paved it/
Bear Bryant won it/
Billy Graham saved it

"SOUTHERN VOICE"
Written by Bob DiPiero and Tom Douglas
Recorded by Tim McGraw for Curb

Bob DiPiero is a gregarious, bigger-than-life bear of a man, and Tom Douglas is deep and introspective. Both are successful, highly regarded songwriters, with writing styles as different as their personalities. And they don't typically write together, but when they got together for this one, they came up with a southern anthem for our time. "Smooth as a hickory wind that blows from Memphis down to Apalachicola," the chorus goes, a major Tim McGraw hit that's chock-full of regional people and places. What better southern quartet of characters could be assembled than a rock star from Florida, a Civil Rights icon from Georgia, the head coach of the most famous football team in Alabama and a legendary North Carolina–born saver of souls who walked this earth for almost one hundred years?

Where were you when the world stopped turning?

"WHERE WERE YOU (WHEN THE WORLD STOPPED TURNING)"
Written by Alan Jackson
Recorded by Alan Jackson for Arista Nashville

Most everyone who was over five or six years old on September 11, 2001, probably remembers what he or she was doing on that fateful day. I was wondering why I was waking up to thirty phone calls on my caller ID, and when my stepson called to ask about my daughter, who was then living in Manhattan ("Haven't you heard that New York was attacked?" he asked), I was half crazy with worry until I found an e-mail from her telling me that she and her husband were okay. Alan Jackson had gone for a walk, and he saw the news on TV when he returned home. He wanted to write an apolitical song about how the news hit everyday Americans. After writing it a few weeks later, he was at first reluctant to record it, not wanting to exploit a national tragedy, but his wife and producer both urged him to. The executives at his record label were stunned when they heard it. He was scheduled to sing his recent hit "Where I Come From" on the CMA Music Awards show on CBS, but then his manager played his recording of "Where Were You" for the top CMA officials and by the end of the song they were all crying. When Alan introduced the song to America via TV on the night of November 7, it was an immediate hit and became the country's healing anthem. I know of no other song about any national event that ever had such an impact. I usually tell my associate Carmen Beecher exactly what I envision for each illustration in this book, but I asked *her* to choose something for this song. She drew a lone fireman in the Twin Towers rubble, his head bowed in prayer, symbolic of the brave first responders, many of whom were among the nearly three thousand murdered by terrorists on what Alan Jackson's powerful song refers to as "that September day."

I remember when the sound of little feet/
Was the music we danced to/
Week-to-week

"REMEMBER WHEN"
Written by Alan Jackson
Recorded by Alan Jackson for Arista Nashville

The wife, children and parents who have frequently appeared in Alan Jackson's songs are thought to be based on his own family. With strong but simple words, a haunting, a majestic melody and his sincere singing style, this 2003 Jackson hit paints a portrait of special bygone moments. I asked Carmen to illustrate a tall country singer, seeing old memories like old movies as he sings his song. I was moved by her added dramatic touch: the singer performing before an audience of thousands as sweet familial scenes play out in his mind's eye.

No shoes, no shirt,/
No problems

"No Shoes, No Shirt, No Problems"
Written by Casey Beathard
Recorded by Kenny Chesney for Universal

Kenny Chesney wasn't exactly an overnight success. Troy Tomlinson signed him as a songwriter to Acuff-Rose Publishing in the early 1990s. Within a year or so, he had a record deal. In the latter half of the 1990s, he started having some hits. By the 2000s, almost ten years after he signed his writing deal, he had become country's biggest celebrity. In fact, Kenny Chesney was so hot that he was promoting two kinds of music: mainstream contemporary country and the laid-back good-time music of the sun, sand and sea—kind of a modern-day Jimmy Buffet style with a country twist. A typical example of this suntan serenade came from the pen of twenty-first-century superwriter Casey Beathard. Since this has been listed both as the best line and by the song title, I won't be redundant, so I'll simply say it's the tale of a guy who's barefoot, shirtless and carefree.

The last word in lonesome is me

"THE LAST WORD IN LONESOME IS ME"
Written by Roger Miller
Recorded by Eddy Arnold for RCA

Roger Miller was one of the funniest people I ever met and definitely the quickest. If you tried to keep up with him in clever banter, it was at your own peril. He came to Nashville from Erick, Oklahoma, and by his early twenties he was a successful hit songwriter. In 1964, he recorded an album of his own songs for Smash Records, and soon he was one of the hottest country and pop artists in America, even landing his own network TV show and, eventually, writing the music for a major Broadway play. There were many big hits, like "King of the Road," but I thought his most clever one was his 1966 Eddy Arnold hit, "The Last Word in Lonesome Is Me." Roger died way too young, and I thought of him often over the years. Early one evening in 2003, I found myself sitting in the parking lot of my neighborhood Kroger grocery in Nashville, waiting for a heavy rain to stop before going into the store. While staring at the Kroger sign, it hit me: "The last word in Kroger is Roger!" Wishing Roger were alive so I could share this with him, I later called his son, Dean, and told him my Kroger/Roger pun. It got a big laugh. "Dad would have loved that," he said.

When you can't save yourself
You save somebody else
Maybe that's how you survive
I'm runnin' away so she don't have to see
A life in slow-motion suicide
You throw in the towel, they call you a coward
Tell ya fight, don't cut and run
I ain't no hero, but the truth is I know
It's the bravest thing I've ever done
The hardest part is knowing
What we could have, should have become
I ain't ever goin'
I ain't ever goin'
I ain't ever goin'
Back there again
No one's gonna make me
Nothing's gonna take me
I ain't ever goin'
To break her heart again

"Back There Again"
Written by Tom Douglas
Recorded by Blake Shelton for Warner

There are two ways that "Back There Again" is not typical of the way the other songs are featured in this book. First, instead of focusing on one line, the song is so powerful lyrically that I'm focusing on the entire last half, which is filled with great lines. Second, this was not a hit single; in fact, it wasn't a single at all. Some great songs aren't—that's just the way it goes sometimes. "Back There Again" was on the first session Blake Shelton ever did that I didn't produce, after working with him for so many years. Paul Worley was the producer, and the song was written by the great Tom Douglas. This was shortly after the breakup of Blake's first marriage, and he totally identified with these words. I wasn't there, but I read somewhere that when he heard the playback of his riveting performance, he broke down and cried. The first line of the song draws you in: "This old Buick's like the needle on a compass pointed due west." Leave it to Tom Douglas.

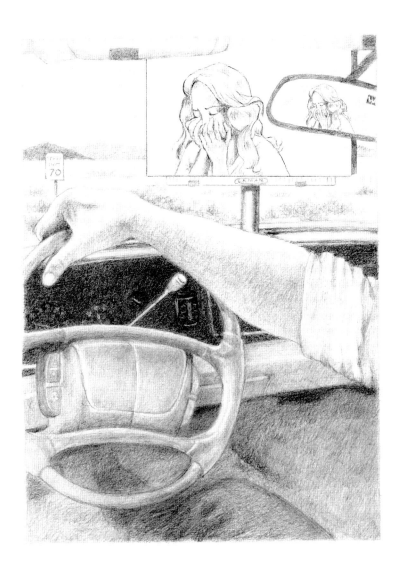

You went away./
How dare you?

"OVER YOU"
Written by Blake Shelton and Miranda Lambert
Recorded by Miranda Lambert for Sony

When they were partners in marriage and music, Blake Shelton and Miranda Lambert wrote "Over You," inspired by the memory of a fourteen-year-old Blake losing his big brother and hero, Richie, in a car accident. I often heard Blake speak of his sibling and how he was influenced by Richie's cassette collection. I think of that when I hear the line, "You sing along with every song." But in all the years I worked with Blake as his producer, I never heard him talk about the death itself. I think writing the song made it easier for him to do that. According to Wikipedia, Miranda said of "Over You," "Blake said he couldn't record it for himself or sing it onstage every night, but he would be honored for me to." Her recording sold nearly 1.4 million downloads, and Blake and Miranda won both the CMA and ACM Song of the Year awards. "You went away. How dare you? I miss you. They say I'll be OK, but I'm not ever going to get over you."

You made a rebel of a careless man's careful daughter,/
You are the best thing that's ever been mine

"MINE"
Written by Taylor Swift
Recorded by Taylor Swift for Big Machine

The first time I met Taylor Swift was on her seventeenth birthday, December 13, 2006, at a reception celebrating former Beegee Barry Gibb's move to Nashville. I had seen her on TV singing her first hit, "Tim McGraw," and I was thinking that there was no way this teenager would have any idea who I was. But she did and started reeling off a list of my songs. She impressed me, as she did everyone else on Music Row. In no time, this tall, cute, bubbly girl became a popular part of the country music community and a generous and well-respected citizen of Nashville. Even in those earlier years, before she became a strictly pop megastar, some of the older country music fans felt she was too pop for country. But she was an artist/writer whose songs came from the heart and were based on her own true-life experiences. What could be more country than that?

Romeo save me, they're trying to tell me how to feel

"LOVE STORY"
Written by Taylor Swift
Recorded by Taylor Swift for Big Machine

Taylor Swift's second album, *Fearless*, debuted in November 2008, shortly before her nineteenth birthday. It was her first #1 pop album and would eventually sell nearly 9 million worldwide—pretty amazing for the era of declining album sales. The first single, "Love Story," was another #1 country record and her first Top 5 pop single. For the video, a strikingly handsome young dude was hired to play Romeo, and Taylor was beautiful as Juliet. Although older country fans complained that Taylor was too pop, the fact is that she brought her millions of mid-teen female fans into the world of country music.

The sharp knife/
Of a short life

"IF I DIE YOUNG"
Written by Kimberly Perry
Recorded by The Band Perry for Republic Nashville

They seemingly came from out of nowhere in 2010: Kimberly Perry, her brothers Neil and Reid and their pop, rock and bluegrass brand of country. "If I Die Young" went to the top of both the country and adult contemporary charts and to #14 on the pop charts, with certification of 6 million downloads. My impression was "nice kids with a lot of talent." (I did some songwriting with the brothers, and when I met big sister, she was excited about writing a song with one of her idols, Sheryl Crow.) Kimberly's story of mortality, "If I Die Young," seems to me like a young woman's imaginative tale, told in the relative safety of her young years. One hopes that the heroine of her song (and the kitten in Carmen's illustration) somehow escapes the jaws of death and finds the way back home.

*The devil, man, no, he don't stand a chance,/
Cause she loves me like Jesus does*

"LIKE JESUS DOES"
Written by Casey Beathard and Monty Criswell
Recorded by Eric Church for Capitol Nashville

A unique star of the 2010s is country music's Eric Church. With rock star presence and alt-meets-traditional sensibilities, Church has been writing and singing unique songs that have gained him a large, enthusiastic following. However, Eric Church didn't have a hand in writing "Like Jesus Does." The song was written by a pair of Music Row hitmakers. The prolific Casey Beathard is the son of NFL Hall of Famer Bobby Beathard and father of Dot recording star Tucker Beathard and San Francisco 49ers quarterback C.J. Beathard. Monty Criswell's hit song list includes the award-winning "I Saw God Today." The protagonist in Beathard and Criswell's song is a well-intentioned sinner, and his lady is his guiding light. "She believes in me like she believes her Bible," he says. She loves her man—like Jesus does.

*Slowly plannin' my survival/
In a three-foot stack of vinyl*

"RECORD YEAR"
Written by Eric Church and Jeff Hyde
Recorded by Eric Church for EMI Nashville

Vinyl records played the music of my life, from my childhood well into adulthood—even when I started buying songs on 8-track and cassettes for my car, letting go only when records left the mainstream marketplace with the coming of CDs. Now vinyl has made an amazing comeback, with several million records sold per year. That's what Eric Church and Jeff Hyde wrote about in this song: girl leaves guy, guy sits around drinking and playing old 45s and albums—he's having a record year. It's a very clever idea, and besides paying tribute to some classic vinyl stars, it has some catchy lines, such as "Your leavin' left me goin' crazy / I'm countin' on a needle to save me." It's also refreshing, in the last half of the 2010s, to hear a song in which the singer (in the old country music tradition) has the humility to sing about being the one who got dumped. With his trademark sunglasses, Eric Church is sort of Nashville's "Mister Cool," not just in appearance but in the substance and depth of his music. In 2016, "Record Year" went to #1. Each year, Church seems to get bigger than the year before. In more ways than one, he's having a record year.

As the darkness descended the desert/
And a bad actor starred in his play

"WHY NOT ME"
Written by Eric Church
Recorded by Eric Church for EMI

For ten minutes on the night of October 1, 2017, a gunman opened fire from his thirty-second-floor hotel suite into a crowd of 22,000 country music concertgoers at the Route 91 Harvest Music Festival on the Las Vegas Strip. The killer fired 1,100 rounds from an automatic weapon, leaving 58 people dead and 546 injured, making it the deadliest mass shooting ever committed by an individual in the United States. Several nights later, Eric Church appeared on the stage of the Grand Ole Opry. Church, usually stoic behind his sunglasses, was emotional as he recalled headlining at the festival two nights before the tragedy and how he looked out on the audience and thought, "This is my crowd. I've been seeing this crowd all year." And then he said, "Forty-eight hours later, that stage where I stood was carnage. These were my people. These were my fans." As he choked back tears, he went on, "What I saw that night in time, it was frozen. There's no amount of bullets that can take it away." He then told about seeing a video of CNN's Anderson Cooper interviewing a young woman whose husband died in her arms that night. They had come to the festival to see the young man's hero, Eric Church. Then Church's voice grew somber as he reflected, "That night something broke in me, and the only way I've ever fixed anything that's broken in me was with music. So I wrote a song." He then sang his tribute to his fans and all the fans who died in Vegas, the song that asks the question, "Why you and why not me?"

I'd hang "hate" so that it can't be heard/
If only I could kill a word

"KILL A WORD"
Written by Eric Church, Luke Dick and Jeff Hyde
Recorded by Eric Church for EMI Nashville

Here's a contemporary country song that is very clever and also very relevant. It's about a guy who would, if he could, "poison *never*," "shoot *goodbye*," "beat *regret*," "pound *fear* to a pile of sand" and "choke *lonely* out" with his bare hands—if only he could kill a word. Some of the powers-that-be can get a little nervous about songs that wander off the beaten path or stir up a little controversy. Apparently, Eric Church, Jeff Hyde and Luke Dick weren't concerned about that when they wrote "Kill a Word." Eric Church gives us a song about a lonely guy listening to old vinyl records, then one about an adult male learning life lessons from his three-year-old and then this one about "hanging hate" so that it can't be heard. It's almost enough to make an old songwriter feel good about the future of country music.

GLOSSARY OF SONGS BY CHAPTER

Chapter 1: 1940s and 1950s

"I'm So Lonesome I Could Cry"—Written by Hank Williams; Recorded by Hank Williams

"Mind Your Own Business"—Written by Hank Williams; Recorded by Hank Williams

"The Tennessee Waltz"—Written by Pee Wee King and Redd Stewart; Recorded by Patti Page and by many, many others

"I Take the Chance"—Written by Charlie Louvin and Ira Louvin; Recorded by The Browns

"Jambalaya (On the Bayou)"—Written by Hank Williams; Recorded by Hank Williams

"Kaw-Liga"—Written by Hank Williams and Fred Rose; Recorded by Hank Williams, by Charley Pride and by Hank Williams Jr.

"All I Have to Do Is Dream"—Written by Boudeleaux Bryant; Recorded by the Everly Brothers

"I Can't Help It (If I'm Still in Love with You)"—Written by Hank Williams; Recorded by Hank Williams

"El Paso"—Written by Marty Robbins; Recorded by Marty Robbins

Chapter 2: 1960s

"Mama Tried"—Written by Merle Haggard; Recorded by Merle Haggard

"I Can't Stop Loving You"—Written by Don Gibson; Recorded by Don Gibson, by Kitty Wells and by Ray Charles

"Hello Walls"—Written by Willie Nelson; Recorded by Faron Young

"I Fall to Pieces"—Written by Hank Cochran and Harlan Howard; Recorded by Patsy Cline

"Crazy"—Written by Willie Nelson; Recorded by Patsy Cline

"The Other Woman"—Written by Don Rollins; Recorded by Ray Price

"Green, Green Grass of Home"—Written by Curly Putman; Recorded by Porter Wagoner and by Tom Jones

"Don't Touch Me"—Written by Hank Cochran; Recorded by Jeannie Seely

"The Chokin' Kind"—Written by Harlan Howard; Recorded by Waylon Jennings and by Joe Simon

"Mary Ann Regrets"—Written by Harlan Howard; Recorded by Burl Ives

"Once a Day"—Written by Bill Anderson; Recorded by Connie Smith

"Sorrow on the Rocks"—Written by Tony Moon; Recorded by Porter Wagoner

"Games People Play"—Written by Joe South; Recorded by Joe South

"King of the Road"—Written by Roger Miller; Recorded by Roger Miller

"Ballad of Forty Dollars"—Written by Tom T. Hall; Recorded by Tom T. Hall

"When I've Learned"—Written by Ray Baker, Buddy Killen and Delbert Whitson; Recorded by Bobby Bare

"She Even Woke Me Up to Say Goodbye"—Written by Doug Gilmore and Mickey Newbury; Recorded by Jerry Lee Lewis

Chapter 3: 1970s

"'Til I Get It Right"—Written by Larry Henley and Red Lane; Recorded by Tammy Wynette

"Why Me"—Written by Kris Kristofferson; Recorded by Kris Kristofferson

"Help Me Make It Through the Night"—Written by Kris Kristofferson; Recorded by Sammi Smith

"Sunday Morning Coming Down"—Written by Kris Kristofferson; Recorded by Ray Stevens and by Johnny Cash

"Is Anybody Going to San Antone"—Written by Dave Kirby and Glenn Martin; Recorded by Charley Pride

"After the Fire Is Gone"—Written by L.E. White; Recorded by Loretta Lynn and Conway Twitty

"The Midnight Oil"—Written by Joe Allen; Recorded by Barbara Mandrell

"Mammas Don't Let Your Babies Grow Up to Be Cowboys"—Written by Ed Bruce and Patsy Bruce; Recorded by Waylon and Willie and by Ed Bruce

"Back When We Were Young"—Written by Tom T. Hall; Recorded by Tom T. Hall

"One Piece at a Time"—Written by Wayne Kemp; Recorded by Johnny Cash

"Last Cheater's Waltz"—Written by Sonny Throckmorton; Recorded by T.G. Sheppard

"Friday Night Blues"—Written by Sonny Throckmorton & Rafe Van Hoy; Recorded by John Conlee

"The Gambler"—Written by Don Schlitz; Recorded by Kenny Rogers

"Break My Mind"—Written by John D. Loudermilk; Recorded by George Hamilton IV and by Vern Gosdin

"Should I Come Home (Or Should I Go Crazy)"—Written by Joe Allen; Recorded by Gene Watson

Chapter 4: 1980s

"Too Many Rivers"—Written by Harlan Howard; Recorded by Brenda Lee and by the Forrester Sisters

"Life Turned Her That Way"—Written by Harlan Howard; Recorded by Mel Tillis and by Ricky Van Shelton

"I Don't Know a Thing About Love" (The Moon Song)—Written by Harlan Howard; Recorded by Conway Twitty

"I Wish I Was Eighteen Again"—Written by Sonny Throckmorton; Recorded by Jerry Lee Lewis and by George Burns

"I May Never Get to Heaven"—Written by Bill Anderson and Buddy Killen; Recorded by Conway Twitty

"Don't You Ever Get Tired of Hurting Me"—Written by Hank Cochran; Recorded by Ray Price and by Ronnie Milsap

"What's Forever For"—Written by Rafe Van Hoy; Recorded by Michael Martin Murphey

"I Wish that I Could Hurt That Way Again"—Written by Don Cook, Curly Putman and Rafe Van Hoy; recorded by T. Graham Brown

"I Tell It Like It Used to Be"—Written by Michael Garvin, Ron Hellard and Bucky Jones; Recorded by T. Graham Brown

"Till I'm Too Old to Die Young"—Written by Scott Dooley, John Hadley and Kevin Welch; Recorded by Moe Bandy

"Famous Last Words of a Fool"—Written by Dean Dillon and Rex Huston; Recorded by George Strait

"All My Exes Live in Texas"—Written by Whitey Shafer and Lyndia Shafer; Recorded by George Strait

"That's All That Matters"—Written by Hank Cochran; Recorded by Mickey Gilley

"Avalanche of Romance"—Written by Bobby Braddock and Rafe Van Hoy; Recorded by Bobby Braddock

"Killin' Time"—Written by Clint Black and Hayden Nicholas; Recorded by Clint Black

Chapter 5: 1990s

"Independence Day"—Written by Gretchen Peters; Recorded by Martina McBride

"You Don't Even Know Who I Am"—Written by Gretchen Peters; Recorded by Patty Loveless

"A Broken Wing"—Written by James House, Phil Barnhart and Sam Hogin; Recorded by Martina McBride

"Shake the Sugar Tree"—Written by Chapin Hartford; Recorded by Pam Tillis

"Walkin', Talkin', Cryin', Barely Beatin' Broken Heart"—Written by Roger Miller and Justin Tubb; Recorded by Highway 101

"Beautiful Fool"—Written by Don Henry; Recorded by Don Henry and by Kathy Mattea

"Don't Tell Me What to Do"—Written by Max D. Barnes and Harlan Howard; Recorded by Pam Tillis

"Little Rock"—Written by Tom Douglas; Recorded by Collin Raye

"Then You Can Tell Me Goodbye"—Written by John D. Loudermilk; Recorded by the Casinos, by Eddy Arnold, by Glen Campbell and by Neal McCoy

"Little Bitty"—Written by Tom T. Hall; Recorded by Alan Jackson

"Husbands and Wives"—Written by Roger Miller; Recorded by Roger Miller and by Brooks & Dunn

Chapter 6: Twenty-First Century

"Southern Voice"—Written by Bob DiPiero and Tom Douglas; Recorded by Tim McGraw

"Where Were You (When the World Stopped Turning)"—Written by Alan Jackson; Recorded by Alan Jackson

"Remember When"—Written by Alan Jackson; Recorded by Alan Jackson

"No Shoes, No Shirt, No Problems"—Written by Casey Beathard; Recorded by Kenny Chesney

"The Last Word in Lonesome Is Me"—Written by Roger Miller; Recorded by Eddy Arnold

"Back There Again"—Written by Tom Douglas; Recorded by Blake Shelton

"Over You"—Written by Blake Shelton and Miranda Lambert; Recorded by Miranda Lambert

"Mine"—Written by Taylor Swift; Recorded by Taylor Swift

"Love Story"—Written by Taylor Swift; Recorded by Taylor Swift

"If I Die Young"—Written by Kimberly Perry; Recorded by The Band Perry

"Like Jesus Does"—Written by Casey Beathard and Monty Criswell; Recorded by Eric Church

"Record Year"—Written by Eric Church and Jeff Hyde; Recorded by Eric Church

"Why Not Me"—Written by Eric Church; Recorded by Eric Church

"Kill a Word"—Written by Eric Church, Luke Dick and Jeff Hyde; Recorded by Eric Church

ABOUT THE AUTHOR

BOBBY BRADDOCK grew up in Florida, traveled the South as a rock 'n' roll musician and became a songwriter in Nashville in the mid-1960s. Many of his songs—such as "D.I.V.O.R.C.E.," "Golden Ring," "Texas Tornado," "Time Marches On" and "I Wanna Talk About Me"—are country music standards. "He Stopped Loving Her Today" has led most surveys as the best country song of all time. In 2001, he embarked on a new career as a producer, discovering singer Blake Shelton and making several #1 records with him. Braddock's most recent #1 composition was in 2009: "People Are Crazy." He has been inducted into the Nashville Songwriters Hall of Fame (1981), Country Music Hall of Fame (2011) and the Songwriters Hall of Fame in New York (2015). He received the BMI Icon Award in 2011 and the ACM Poets Award in 2012. He has received six CMA Song of the Year nominations, winning twice. Bobby Braddock is the only living person to have written #1 country songs in five consecutive decades. He is the author of two published books: *Down in Orburndale* (Louisiana State University Press, 2007) and *Bobby Braddock: A Life on Nashville's Music Row* (Vanderbilt University Press/Country Music Foundation Press, 2015).

ALSO BY BOBBY BRADDOCK:

Bobby Braddock: A Life on Nashville's Music Row
Down in Orburndale: A Songwriter's Youth in Old Florida

ABOUT THE ILLUSTRATOR

CARMEN BEECHER grew up in a tiny Florida town but saw much of the world while working for the U.S. Air Force. She lived in both Bermuda and the Azores Islands for many years, so it is little wonder that her fascination with water is evident in much of her art. She has paintings in the Pentagon's Air Force Art Collection and awards for Air Force Published Graphic Art and Fine Arts Drawing. Retirement from her service job has meant freedom to pursue all forms of art. Her work *River of Tears*, about her father's struggles with alcohol, was selected for exhibition in the Johns Hopkins University School of Medicine Art and Addiction 2008 Juried Art Exhibition and was included in the book *Addiction and Art*. Her freelance work includes book illustrations, comic strips, magazine covers, murals and credit card designs. Her paintings and her process were featured in *International Artist Magazine*. When Bobby Braddock decided he wanted to collaborate with an illustrator for *Country Music's Greatest Lines*, the first person he thought of was Carmen, whom he had known since they were in their teens. "We did it via long-distance calls and e-mails between Tennessee and Florida," said Braddock. "I would tell her what I saw in my mind's eye in great detail, and she would bring it vividly to life, blowing me away every time."

ALSO BY CARMEN BEECHER:

Dibble the Dragon